The Healing Leaf

The Healing Leaf

A Poetry Collection

Pamela Moorehead, Msc.D

Order this book online at www.trafford.com
or email orders@trafford.com

Most Trafford titles are also available at major online book retailers.

Printed in the United States of America.

ISBN: 978-1-4269-7415-1 (sc)
ISBN: 978-1-4269-7416-8 (e)

Trafford rev. 08/06/2012

 www.trafford.com

North America & international
toll-free: 1 888 232 4444 (USA & Canada)
phone: 250 383 6864 ♦ fax: 812 355 4082

To my family and friends with love
Lightening, Mupa, Mr. Brown, Cat Daddy

Acknowledgement

This book is written in honor of all those who I have met and the meeting has changed our lives for the better. While writing this book I would like to give a special thanks to Charles, for keeping me focused spiritually, mentally and physically. Stay in the compassionate way; May your life always be blessed with love peace and prosperity you are an Earth Source.
I would like to thank Pablo, for believing in me no matter what I do; May your life be inspired with inspiration and may all your dreams come true. I would like to say thank you to David, for reminding me of who I truly am and the task I have in front of me; may the Heavenly Hierarchy lead you and embrace you in all that you do

Epitaph

I was a young woman, an aspiring Poet, at a book signing for Pulitzer Prize winner, Phillip Levine, and his wife Frances Levine, I asked the question of author and Poet Phillip Levine, "What does it take to win the Pulitzer Prize?" He answered by writing his advice with his autograph in an Anthology that I had published, "How to win a Pulitzer prize: work and write and then work and write and then be lucky." Frances Levine, listening to the conversation as I was about to have the book signed by her, for her cook book, wrote: "Best wishes and good luck!

I thought at that time, the right ingredients, love always being a major ingredient of any great cook. This was evident in her recipe book for a good marriage synergy.

Elements

Air

The lessons in life where you find freedom by the choices that you have made. Whether it is bad or good, the lessons bring liberation. You must aspire high to attain freedom. When lessons teach you independence in a dependent society you must be as unpredictable as the wind. These lessons from this element it is capable of moving all.

Fire

The lessons will come from impulse and passion. The drive can be found when dealing with problems and lessons of love and hate. These lessons are like the Phoenix, when you fall to the ground you must know that you will rise from the ashes. Be careful with playing with such an unpredictable element especially when mixed with air.

Water

Attitudes and emotions are the lessons that comes from loving. Or, what happens from the lack of knowing the power of love. That is why it is so hard for some people to believe or trust others. It seems as allusive as water when it slips through your fingers. Not learning what love truly is and to consider how to love and be loved. This can create instability and a barren desert. It is also the formation of the planet earth and all that survive upon the planet. It is the replenisher of spiritual bareness.

Earth

You will receive the lessons of earth consequence. You will learn that there is only a function no larger than the world in which you need to reside. Besides the world you live in, there is a longing for a brighter future. Stability and function are the lessons achieved. Organization, skill, responibility and courage are attained. This is where we choose our mask for the physical presentation that house the spirit. Our mask can show the affects that life has upon the dusty rags, or clay.

Ethereal

The fifth element that which is Ethereal. When conciousness of self is felt separately from the masses and yet it still feels part of the whole, it is a paradox. It represents perfect balance and love. When securely claimed you surrender to the pure will of Omnipotent perfection. Coming from the Creator, that makes us as perfect as we can be. Declare the facts, when truth is your essence power is with you at all times. Omnipotent power declare judgment and release the Will. The scales of justice and blindness when implemented carry the weight of righteousness. But know we are in this world not of this world. We are humane entities. We are a masterpiece within ourselves. It is a peace of true mastering that which controls us when we are out of control. The magic of communication, forgiveness and love, we are ethereal. One day we are released from the body in truth and acceptance of that realness.

Achieving the goal

When all elememts become balanced, there is achievement when light is shed upon truth. The more you know the true history, the better chances a man has not to repeat the mistakes of the past. He learns the mistakes from the past become too costly. We are to take the positive from our life lessons, figure out the negative experiences and leave them behind. Yet keep a mental journal of what doesn't belong in your atmosphere.

Figure out what doesn't fit your life path and put it all into perspective. The great masters of poetry, Scientist and those of the various arts, have known this balance at some point. They make you feel and think. The realization of what we become in life is placed in a mirror in front of us. That is good unless we look into that mirror and it is distorted. We have the potential to learn from all human behavior. Our experiences alone, or the intermingling with others create cause and affect. And the pendulum affect that life has a rhythm and timing.

Depending on how honest you can be with yourself and others, will determine what kind of relationship there will be. There will be less conflict dealing with other people when we stay in reality. Being Judge is not our job. We are charged to gather the facts and proceed to bring back ethics and morals. They have been tossed aside in a decaying world that has not been able to grasp the importance of a society with scruples. Whether we choose to love with all our heart or not, remember the light is all we take with us to the transformation.

A healthy life style is required to enjoy life too the fullest. The love of poetry can help heal the mind, body, and spirit. Everyone who read or write a poem can share what they feel, think or learn from poetry. Poems have the power to inspire your feelings, and compell you to spill your life upon the ready pages of your mind like indellible ink. Communication is very important. Beauty is the function when you express yourself and say something. This heals or at least bring about a better understanding. Temperance and harmony will unite us by understanding.

The Introduction of metaphysical Poetry the Science of word and the vocal vibration

This book of poetry is a metaphysical scientific literature. The intergration of the Poet and the reader, dealing with the controvertial, or uncomfortable moments in life. Teaching how to dump or leave traumatic or hurtful times in your life two blocks behind. Stay in the moment, move forward and release plenty of stress. The need of reading the Healing Leaf, and gaining an understanding of different perceptions on complicated issues. Take positive all of the suggested methods of using the vocal vibrations and embrace love, As humanity we are as independent as we are a whole. The roles we play in each others' lives and the outcome of the situation affects us all if we are honest about our interactions. My work as a Metaphysician, is to help all embrace, find their connection to the spoken and written word humanity responds to these experiences.

The wailing (welling) wall provided for your opportunity to work poisons or dross out of your system. Allowing the reading of the poems to permeate your being. The writing on the wall, the pages left blank to express the feelings and thoughts helps to heal. You get to acknowledge what attitude and emotion are you holding? Any attitudes and emotions that affect our mind, body and spirit are contagious. Until mankind makes a conscious application of the alignment of the Will, (wheel) to our choices and the long term affects of our decisions.

It is not my intention to insult, hurt, or harm anyone. Communication is a craftful skill. If they would like to place themself as the character at that period of time. Others in the field of medicine Holistic or otherwise knows that quantum physically manipulating the body in a less invasive method. When those medical invasive methods of surgery are necessary it is important to strengthen your body, mind and spirit.

I agree with Dr. Edgar Cayce, that when the psychological, spiritual and physical healing doctors work in unison measures, medicine will become more proficient, proactive, preventative, medicine. Rehabilitation and the health of the individual can all be under one accord, and that is the well being of the patient. And life expectancy and quality of living shall rise and mankind can utilize his inner strength, energies and utilize the importance of prana to intake the proper nutrients.

To heal and change one another until there is a new Jerusalem. A four square city with walls of peace abound humanity again. The circle is complete and the garden will be in our lives one step at a time.

Along with the observation and thoughts of the author, in the future book, "One plus One makes Two." Why our children believe cheating is as good as studying and hard work, and the truth is the same as a lie. We are capable of recognizing the importance of being capable of doing the best work. And fast food represents I get what I want now, I shouldn't earm it nor get it when I can handle it. Young people say they are doing what they see and learn from those that are older and have sat the example.

Inducting the Prana

Instructions

1. When reading this book of poetry take the words into your mouth and eat them as if it were the finest chocolate. Digest them into your mind. Then allow them to flow all through your being until you feel what the author feels or what you feel. Maybe you have had some of these experiences yourself, if not empathy helps us to better understand it will rid one of toxins and fill that void with a positive element that is needed whether it

2. Swallow; that is, to allow your mind and emotions to come in contact to what you are truly taking into your mind and pay attention to your perception of the words used. Its affect upon you totally.

3. Meditate upon the fact of what you are being asked to do as you read so that your mind stays focused on the method that you are utilizing. In other words to eat one must chew taste and swallow, Metaphors for the art of reading

4. What do you feel in your heart? In those five secret chakra chambers where your true feelings reside.

5. The vocal vibration pattern that opens those chakras upon healing to radiate those light forces that give what we say you can be yourself.

6. Pull into your third eye the trust following your true feelings to make the right decisions and know that any decision you make affect everyone and everything and entity around you.

7. Now take the knowledge that comes to you from your highest being and elevate your mind to the highest vibratory state and write upon the wailing wall the feelings of your journey within the written words of these poem

The Healing Leaf

Each poem is written from the authors experience whether her own or those who participated in the educational room of this experience called "life". There are those moments when your attitudes and emotions whether positive or negative brings you to your freedom. Like a butterfly changing from a catepillar shedding its caccoon into a beautiful species. One of the signatures of the healer from ancient times was this symbol of the butterfly. One reason for this is because its transformation is a symbol of our transition.

Also, It is because there is vibratory force in everything. As you eat these words think about the power that is being released and orchestrated in unison with your chakras. Liquility of the body men's state of the minerals, radiates from us in the same manner energy is released from minerals. People share energy amongst each other like crystals. Some block, some purge, some heal in many powerful ways, physical, mental and spiritual necessities.

Prana or energy is released at various vibratory rates from 144,000 chakra points with seven main relative chakra points. To some it may feel like inertia, to some the feel the strong vibration of movement. There are the four basic elements air, fire, water, and earth, the fifth is ethereal.

Love

If I give nothing else allow me to share the love that I have with you. There are many situations taking place in our life daily. When we engage with other facets of our perceptions always trying to please. That which is not true can only cause a dis-ease. We should know the value of character and let the light shine.

Some things must be priceless, for it is rare and to share it amongst each other we well our familiars. The ability to utilize the strength to enhance every organism seen and unseen. By want of participation in this life time. No matter what choices we make know that we have participated. Think about sitting on the sidelines. That it self is a choice? What I am saying is that the responsibility of words, and the response is huge in the outcome of the conversation.

The collectioon of poems should spark the conversation, But do not run from them. It is a time for healing. Because whatever you decide there is a choice you have made. Let it be for the uplifting of a broken country. That has needed to be fixed for a long time. Stay in reality, some might say what is reality? That is why we must stay within the boundaries of justice, temperance, respect, honor and love. These are foundation to reality. All that stay within the boundaries of love, not making it what we want love to be. But, what love is and how valuable this concept is, because there would be less waste and less hate. If wickedness turn you on, be honest enough to tell yourself why. Also, tell others, so that the lessons to be learned come not as a destraction to self. Be honest for clarity to be given to others. Because there will be a dis-ease response that contradict that which is not true. It will be destructive for that is the nature of its being.

Meditate on this job, it is work to give love to thought that would seem useless at this time. Believe that it is important for every moment that we become the people that we say we are by mouth. We live it in our daily walk. To truly use your own mind and not allow others to make the decision to think for you. Exercise your mind as well as your body and spirit in the manner that complements. Allow without judgement and remember the gathering of facts is not judgment. Judgement is rendered after the verdict. Beyond a reasonable doubt, without prejudice but justice. Facts based on a persons own merit. That is why there has to be a Wise entity that sits in that seat and the Grand seat in the Universe.

Eat these words as if you are eating for survival because you are. Stay in reality even when it seems all is falling apart around you. Trust in that which has made all of this possible and ask yourself how big without life are we really. That life is seen in the prana of all living creatures.

The Uncomfortable Conversation (America) would it be easier for us to have the conversation of racism if we pretended we were all the same color? Would that resolve the issue? Then what would be the reason for prejudice? Would it be religion? Yes, it is also a problem for some people now. Would it be cast, culture, within the same race would it be the variation or color tone? How about language? Does blue blood determine privilege? What kind of privilege? It always has, because of the capability and power to own whatever money could buy. We all know that there are many reasons for humanity to create differences amongst each other.

The absolute truth, we all know that we are to feel great about ourselves. There is a problem when we take those great feelings and use them to attempt to take from the value of other people that we are to have everything that is valuable and good. If we determine that others do not fit within our world because the rules we create to do this, should not we be wise enough to question what we are doing? We respect each other for the position we have or the jobs we do. I believe this can happen without placing another human being beneath our feet to make ourselves feel good.

Remember the show,"Gilligan's Island." There were all caucasian people. A captain of the ship, crew member, professor, movie star, a millionaire couple, and the girl next door. People of different status in life, wealth versus poverty, beauty versus average, intelligence versus lack of intelligence end up on a deserted island without nothing and no one to determine a difference between any of the castaways but them? In that time a person of color would probably be the maid, or the cook, let me be honest to say, that person would have been the slave. This is Americas history and once Barrack Obama, became President, all thought the conversation would automatically become easy but it didn't.

This long established division and crafty placement of people of color and various cultures in America, has not helped our country at all. "A house divided cannot stand." Who are we if our actions which apply ethics, morals, boundaries, understanding, and forgiveness. If there is a catastrophe, and there is no looting shown on the monitor. And a journalist on television tells the story of total devastation. Catastrophe hits, your hands are out for help.

This is all over the world. Depending on the color of the people will they show looting, like Katrina.

No one is coming, even when they see you are needy. They keep going, days go by, you are hungry and thirsty, no one is around. The store is not in operation, the windows are blown out life as you know it may be over. Would you go in the market and get clean water and food? If your children were hungry any mother or father would answer, "I must take care of my children." Perhaps you'd leave money, write a note letting the owner, or owners know what you took some items that your family need to survive. But keep in mind you have no idea what is truly taking place in the world . How many people are living? Remember all the devastations that have taken place in the last twenty years? Look back on the selection of what was shown by different media outlets and how they chose to show different people. Black people, looters, white people take because of need, or it is not shown.

Other people around the world will select what will be shown in the media as to how it will be taken by the rest of the world. I can comfortably say that people of color many times receive a terrible rap. Over the years innocent men have been charged with rape because family members couldn't accept their children being seen with other people of color. Or, like in Tulsa, Oaklahoma, The influential blacks, had too much money as entrepreneurs so they created trouble to go to the areas where they had attained their riches and destroy it and steal it. That blacks were put in Encampments for long periods of time as if they were the people whom created the trouble. They were determined to end the madness in the most wicked manner. Property has been taken, virtually stolen because they may have inherited property, but because they are not legally savy, or book smart they were taken advantage of in some of the most criminal ways.

There are attorneys that do not want to represent them because they do not have the money that they want to charge them, or they will charge an amount that will be costly to make it hard to achieve what is necessary. I could go on forever, but I do not have to tell anyone the no coloreds allowed sign has not been that long being taken down. after slavery, slavery continued in many ways. People will say,"we have a black President, there is no racism", when are people willing to be honest enough to say, I am racist and I like things the way they are, even if the black people must suffer or continue living the life they live, tough!

A divided house cannot stand, America wake up. Lies, cheating, sociopathic or psychopathic behavior, sexuaul deviance, and drugs are all the affects of hate and entitlement. I speak for all people whose civil rights are violated, that would include causasian people whom are persecuted for fighting for the injustice. Some are looked at as if they are an outcast not as important as some others. what is sad is people because of old and passed down behaviors do not stop it stunts the growth of the tree. Remember these poems are experiences whether they are metaphors used or placed in poetic form there is true stories within them.

Man has been evolving since the beginning of time. Transitioning since the waters parted from to the Alpa and the Omega, from the beginning to the end.

Contents

The Artist

I am a painter
I take the words of time
and express what I have experienced
in some point of this era in miming

and others that have bared
their soul passionately rhyming
making the portrait
that perfection unfold
the periods of history clearer

On the prepared canvas dearer
vision inspired tempered colors
Heavenly imposed I show
my courage and let go
of my thoughts and feelings

feelings that seem to flow
I dip my finger tips
in the color on the palate and chose
ostentatious my medium of choice

At other times I soften
the pictures of my voice
using pen and ink
As visual
as the individuals I've known

the power of the pen
as a lethal weapon
chosen as the words

Electronically provoked
by the time we live in

Here upon the planet earth
Keeping the arts alive
constantly adds to mirth
every poem created
is like a new birth

A powerful flip of the wrist
Intoxicating displaying
quantum moments with a twist
Poetry that lingers into
the sentiment of mind

stunning images lucid as its kind
struck by the sensation
of showmanship I find
integrates the need of gratitude
and honor that kindle fonder

That give to all of the ages
pieces of the artist
at talent's various stages
Art impressed indelible
in others from Moor head

the merriment of prose inclined
rhythm and rhyme not blind
dipping the hairs of the brush
into quirkiness instead dripping
the blood sweat and tears

1

that falls into the paint
Wondering if this will be one
or the next one that is done
Does it hold the Labradorite
as I lightly stroke the paper

with astonishing delight
it stirs a freedom so bright
to paint on the canvas
as fast as fire simple
yet sometimes not so easy

when night lay on day light
skill patience and intuition
gives way to write
a stroke of luck in sight
will end my vigorous plight

render a beautiful way to say
we can build skyscrapers
in the same way
but we do not want to play
I pray for a masterpiece

The Eye of the Storm

Today I sit in the eye of the storm
on such a dark and cloudy day
perhaps gray rest upon my heart
the poor child they took away
Just the other day someone lied
others died some were born on that
day

But in Tucson Arizona a young girl
is put to rest
born 9/11/2001 'til 12/07/2011
And now she lay
Out of the Eye of the storm
the cherubim came

Ether passed unsuspecting faces
touching them as they rush
to give a precious stones
with the true name
the father knows
precious life and angels

escort and take good souls
that is the freedom
the spirit that gives
a lesson if we take it
and hold on

Her beautiful lips
that pursed themselves
to exclaim of humanity
all her plans
and bring changes someday
and lived life to the fullest

in the shortest grand display
She has brought changes
along with the others
who were injured
and slaughtered and sacrificed
for all to see we must change

our vocal cords that vibrations
are positive and happy
not hateful spiteful wicked evil
disruptive political war mongers
who put prices
upon innocent heads

we give up so many good kids
our future corruptly dead
We will keep screaming at society
until somebody sees us
We will keep whispering at society
so that maybe they'll finally hear us

We cannot afford to have foolish
people in politics
to lead us with no empathy
or remorse profile it or ponder
knowing that words
are persuasive powerful weapons

pointed with deception
Taking life as you're the victim
as if your rights are taken
you need to stop faking
so good politicians can be
reawakened
that we as a people do have hope

that is why we turn out
to the booths and vote
You are in politics understanding
that your word is sharp

in representation to put
your ideas and thoughts

objectively and subliminal
upon the masses
If America is truly
"land of the free
and home of the brave"
these words I'm saying

should not be a call to put
your loved ones in the grave
A loving heart can only feel
compassion for the foolish
I understand how people
believe in a topsy turvy world

that need to be seen
as ghoulish and Brutus
But a real leader is not
a follower so what excuses
do you have now
I love my country

I pray for my country
and I'll pray to stay bigger
than you somehow
I've seen you before
and I've felt you before
in the eye of the storm

You freed courageous
honorable people that day

Believing you killed them
no, their spirit wait at the gate
powerful and vigorous Fate!

Edgar

My feathered friend
A crow as black
and beautiful as the night
not Edgar Allen Poe
although that was
his name as a crow
A work in flight

the most human like
crow craw sounds
and english language wow
like the walk-ins
my people spoke of
long ago and Figero
my grandmother's
minor bird talked so

who talked out loud
Edgar was the mascot
of Vinland Elementary school
no, they did not buy him
he was wild and one day came
like a stranger into
the neighborhood
he would hang around
the playground and live
in the trees

of the the surrounding
neighborhoods

They say crows
like shiny objects
and will steal your food
My daughter was playing
at school one day
and told Edgar she
didn't feel like playing
"just go away you"

Did I foget to mention
that edgar wasn't
just a bird supernatural
For over eighteen years
in the neighborhood
he convinced us
who he Edgar truly was

a walk-in known
by the ancients
he made my daughter
understand him well
everyday after that
he would peck or chase
her if he could
Everyone knew him

in the area
the mean kids
would swing the bat
that is how I met Edgar
saving him from

the neighborhood brats
they were annoyed by him

that was very clear
But that doesn't give
the children the right
to kill him for sharing
their lunch or demanding
attention from them
Edgar would be
in the tree

and as I passed he'd say
"How are you doing?
Where are you going?
What's your name"
I know that birds can talk
but not a wild bird
that flys everywhere

he wasn't constantly trained
pampered for and cared
He'd follow me
and my children
when we would walk
to the corner store
he'd also fly
and walk us back

like a protector
to our house door
In the morning
at 5:00am or 6:00am
he'd be walking

along the sidewalk
As if he were like

the rest of us
who excercised by walking
around the block
Believe me it was't often
that he'd not just squawking
he would also be talking
One morning
in my daughters room

the window was wide open
we had the music
playing loud and guess
who invited himself
over to party
Edgar was on
the window sill

bouncing and yoking
his head to the sound
of music
If other people hadn't seen
all these things you'd say
they'd think
what an imagination
you would tell me

to go get checked out
before I ruin my reputation
One day my daughter
saw Edgar coming
he had been bothering

5

her all day
so she ran down

the middle of the street
looking like the movie
from the black and white
Alfred Hitchcock movie
it was strange
He then decided to pick
on my youngest he
was five at this time

He didn't have anything
on shiny so he decided
to do it for no
reason or rhyme
One day I told him
"edgar you better leave
my children alone"

My mother told me
that I should have
cooked him in a pot
and boiled him to the bone
He layed his head
to the side he understood
everything that I said
We were on the play ground

as he looked at me
from the swing seat
I stood there and told him
give me his best
and he put me to the test

He came flying towrd me
and I peacefully waved my hands

slowly in front of myself
Edgar flew past me
and flew to the branch
of the tree and looked
at me with respect
He never bothered
my children again
we kept our friendship

Then I did not see
him for a while
I wondered if he was dead
Before I knew it
months had passed by
I knew I would hear
what I did not want

to hear that some human viciously
finally killed him
and sat his soul free
Now the native american
family say
he was a spirit
that shifted himself that way
for omens and guides

protection he chose
certain people
by the aura he sees
That light would shine
brighter than any man made

so they choose the people he
paths cross purposely

Until this day my children
friends family neighbors
and acqaintences
say how much we miss
his physical being
Edgar whatever dimension
your soul was released
in your presence

Why?

Why must we suffer?
It seems to be a partner
with pain
must there always be
sacrifice to realize
all we have to gain
stand up

for what we believe in
what we know is right
If we do not have
a moral fortitutde
we could be sold
for any price
accept the ethical compass

of those ships
that has crashed

not fail to remember
history's creations
because we are living
them today
so we must plant strength

in our garden of determination
the advance of common sense
for us to have a better
tomorrow
today we must plant the seeds
of intelligence and success
Get our heads

back into reality
Know that our voices
need to be heard
rid ourselves
of our sorrows
forcefully move
to do our best

those votes do count
they do make a difference
we must stand strong
in our vigilance
people died
to get these rights
let no one deceive you

of the plight
that there was not
victory with that fight

for the first time
I am truly
working with democracy
speaking in the ears

of Washington, D.C.
people being called upon
we are making the history
democracy works
when the Commander and Chief
keeps his promise when he says
I'm in the seat but I work for the
public
its we not me we must finish
what we started to stay free

Better Understanding

There is a strain
in my heart for humanity
We speak with our tongues
as how we view insanity
Turn around and the actions
are not noble gestures
Violence sex drugs
and alcohol are our pleasures

Somehow mankind cannot
get it together
Now I cannot say
that I am perfect

as a child in our time
was truly worth it

If we have become
honest about loving
and living bullying from
every perpetrator would
disintegrate into
nothing

to see others suffer
then I suggest we stop
pampering ourselves
and get a bit tougher
and then why didn't we
keep it sweet and real

What if anything
life means something
That we did not
end up here on a fluke
And that there is God
in Heaven and you

Sipped the yak
just like poignant gruel
Gain a better understanding
call no man a fool
common sense is measured
as a hidden treasure
What could be better than a
better understanding

Frustration

Why do people have problems
listening to other people
they do not understand?
Why do they take
the words of those
who see the world
so wickedly claimed

They do not want
to talk about others
but talk about
others all the same
why do people side
with some and not others
without knowing the truth?

Because that is
what they choose
because it fits their purpose?
Is that person
so irritating to them
they cannot see that
the people are talking?

about themselves?
Isn't gossiping about others
and why cannot
that person talk
about self?
because they usually do
how about you?

Unless they have something to
really say but they do not
want it exposed that way
so they will talk about others
perhaps even stutter
for they do not feel comfortable
telling anything about them

When the Saints
Go Home

It is a true feeling
of greatness
to be in the
company of saints
some say men
make Saints
Or those of the
spirit of Christ

well some say
these persons
must have documented
two miracles
and pass through
a committee of men
doctors scientist
and religious leaders

here on earth
to make this decision
the Pope of the catholic church
must sign it

and by his affirmation
the person becomes a
Saint
but whom stands

bold as a Saint
put here by God
a holy person
As a holy man
annoited by God
awed by all churches
Or annoited by God
through circumstance

It is compelled
too be done
who becomes a Saint
hero by exemplifying virtue
faith and miracles
work in his or her religion
sanctus holy one
those gone unknown

by man only those
who look whom seek
the virtues of the many
deeds one has done
no matter how big or
how small with God
judgemnt is thine
have you seen it all?

A Saint of this kind
did this Saint ever fulfill
your need to rid of hunger
did you need encouragement
and comfort to fill and empty
soul and supernatural experiences
with joy and laughter

carry you when
you couldn't go on
was this Saint someone
who warmed your spirit
told you what he or she thought
you could bare to hear
saved you from the
two edged sword

when you were weak
when the Saint's are weak
when they show
their human spirit
wrestle with the truth
when the truth
wasn't in it
I have known Saints

and I am not
looking for man
to prove this
in my heart
I know this is where
the truth is

for as she loved
to say we are dirty rags

that shall be shed one day
we are souls on earth
moved by the spirit
we all know where
the Saint's are
at sometime or another
we have all bared witness
to their kindness

there are the many of us
who know
Our matriarch
our greatgrandmother
our grandmother our mother
Queen of Hearts
this day I celebrate
your home going

I give honor to your name
I praise God Heavenly
Father of Jesus christ
who died for our sins
thank you for allowing
me to see this day
I pray to see you in
the after life again

Dear Grandmother:

When I wake up in the morning
And see the sun
it reminds me of
the blaze I see in your eyes

I see the stillest waters
from the ancient one
From the Alpha to the Omega
the serpent eating its tail

Beginning of creation
and birth in the Shadow valley
The lines on your face
show the rivers you crossed

So many times
since your being
They are the medals of courage
when time wanted to stay

And capture your spirit
Tired but willing
You keep going
to show your true feelings

In your smile I see
all the hope of what I can be
All that you know I am
your mind reminds me of every

color of the sky
Many facets of a diamond
many trinkets of stories
Old and new loss and glory

How dare they underestimate
the determination in you
Your soul is awesome
it's splendid wonder in review

Couldn't make me any fonder
of this woman strong limb
That has so much love
too let it flow

Let not your giving
have been in vain
Let not the love I feel for you
be cast upon the rocks

like ocean waves
Tears for you truly
represented all these years
A universe of what a true

grandmother should be like
When you cross
to the other side
(written after death next line)
Now that you crossed
to the other side

Please say a prayer for us
and keep us in your eyes

As you walk you talk with God
full of purpose full of joy

Full of laughter sometimes coy
I'll look around and
I'll see you these
I'll look around as you dance

at my wedding
Today I dance for you
for you dressed
for the Bride's Groom

All the philosophical advice
the hurtful sayings you soothed
with kindness
In my heart to take

to the grave that be
The roots that are binding
they bind me freely
to you the Elder

A million tears

I have cried a million tears
and after all these years
the love I feel inside
the memories not denied
I cannot hide from me

it is faith that set me
free from the pain

that wants me to be saved
I've waved the magic wand
and a new life has begun

a future full of love
show mercy from
constellations above
sweet victory is my name
a new world is my claim

I'll open up my heart
to fill the empty carts
of broken hearted larks
the illusions glow of love
sweet music fill all ears

no more worries
no more cares
and after all these years
I've cried a million tears
for the world

2 the hearts of men

Do you really know
the person you are with
or do you believe
all you see is what you get

Sometime we believe we
know ourselves
and ask others for a description
but the picture isn't self

Get to know the hearts
of men they will steal
your wealth you make you think
you have nothing

But remember you have you
and all that you do
and the things within your mind
the people you may find

hearts may be corrupt
or users for a buck
killers or lovers but
we must discover
2 get to know the hearts of men

Sometimes these hearts are good
Just like there is bad in the world
know that there is good
Know you are not the only one

We Pluck

We pluck
what we want
from the grass
it does not matter
if we need it or not

we pluck
because we do not
know any better
that some things

13

should be left alone

we pluck
because we look around
we want our own
and play keep up
with the Jones
because another has one
we pluck

we pluck
because we dream
of what they have
What we want

we pluck
because we do not
recognize what we have
and find satisfaction inside
we pluck

we pluck
when we do not
acknowledge why
we pluck What luck!

A Play On Words

In the mystic's vision flight
I learned of you
and loves true plight
A man as gentle as a storm
Could spark my fire within

his arms and his charm

Unspoken words
spoken so loudly
I couldn't hear myself think
Then Down the corridor
of my mind this thief of hearts
Against the tide cast his net
I lost my pride

At last, swift upon
the shore
I fight no more
I fight no more
On this train there
will be no polar bears

Only a snake that shed
its skin 'til bare
from here until
eternity's end
Be ye infinite

My love is with my instrument

it seems to pleasure
me as well as others
It is poetry with a twist

If I staged flatly engaged
would you listen to
my happiness and lows

I know by watching
many audiences it takes
a performance to glow

It is beat with a fist
It took sometime for me
to find myself as a musician

But listening to many
greats in acting
music and my fate

it isn't taken light
When one grabs the mike
we must say something

Stained Heart I

What could I have done
but to satisfy my
curiosity for something
or someone different

I would have ran
almost to anyone
or anything to shake
the boughs of love

It had a lock on me
and I almost couldn't
recognize self and could
no longer be selfish

I would not know
me or he or she
There is no greater gift
than love a lover can give

And there is no
greater sacrifice
than to give it up
unconditionally to others

A stained Heart II

there is one heart
with two hands
that has pulled
it in two directions

there is no pain
greater in love than this
because not one
hand will ever be

your's to hold onto
and no kiss past
present or future
can stop the flowing river

that run from
the reserve of my eyes
Love can never be
erased or misplaced

used for any other emotion
A stained heart is
reminded everyday
Wise worth the stain

Anger

I am so angered
tossed about like a passenger
on a cruise ship
on the rolling sea in
the midst of a Tsunami
this terrifies me

I am so sad
I feel I have been had
I laugh and cry to keep
from becoming mad
If in time I gain complete
strength from this affliction

maybe I can move on
with great conviction
But am I caught in the belly
of the whale I cannot tell
these people suppose to be
co-workers, friends and family
not enemies

Meditation

I need to lose me
to sort out this aggravation
I see these were entities
and mere want to be s
they are buzzing puzzled

speaking of my motivation
that drove me too reach out
using my potential lifting
to higher elevation
I find when meditation

Portraits in the mirror reflect back
eyes squint to see them
clearer past the broken glass
wanting too free myself
They live the life that

they perceive of what
this country want them to be
superficial, selfish competitive
too a point that
they are never free

Perhaps the reason haters
hate people like me
is because we look at trees
as living creatures we hear
the butterfly flap its wings

the taste of fresh squeezed
lemonade tart and sweet
Also appreciate the wisdom
of the elderly
and the laughter of babies

First Ray
(the riddle of the Sphinx)

I am Gem In the I of Ra
A riddle of the Sphinx
Princess Woo Le Te Kidane

Woo le te Miskal
Saife Mikal I strike
with the power of lightening

Ra
Osiris was chopped
into how many pieces?
The High Priest held this stone

over Nefertiti's head?
The Moor are known
for this characteristic

Sometimes the hardest
is the most simplistic
Lightening is the beloved
of Ra!

The Gemini

I Am Gem in the Eye
of God!
I affirm my hominid
Slayer of the zodiac
Thoth rules this entity
by mercurial strength
the brilliance of
Simeon and Levi

guard of the gate
influence me taking
that which allows me
to arise to my best
I am tested by
the unrest of chaos
it is my obligation
too extreme regardless
of request

that no matter what part
of the celestial pie
we are from
we all need to balance
our work until the job is done

Friend or Foe
(The biggest smile)

if they are candy
Everything in life has
its lows and its highs

Mine is to question why?
There are days
when my smile shine wide
To disguise what I feel
inside this mortal shell
Most days I don't feel so well
The only thing I can do

is break down and cry
There is a strain on my brain
from all the pain
Acting out the habits
of the insane
When comfort creeps
inside my head
While I am laying
still upon my bed

You see pain knows me
well and I know pain
Pain hasn't been
a good friend to me
More like a foe
a sworn enemy
Many times knowing pain
have wished me dead
A struggling soul must

be led and also fed
Constant faith and hope
to fill one's head
Every time my friend
said I would not last
Tears would flow and I

would clasp my hands fast
Teeth grinding
Forehead frowning

Backstabbing
Burning sensations from
a fire for learning
Seems I'm earning a bad rap
Pain is not my friend
My foe has thrown me in a trap
Bending stiff as
dry willow branches
Pills people wonder

Worried about addiction
worn out petitions
Not the thresh hold
of my conviction
Acute Pain is the assassin
for the disease and injury
of my life Pain is the
Terminator and heartless
is the exterminator

Who shall seek souls

A strike for the soul srike for
the soul there is a strike ...
Lord take away this feeling inside

Something in life is trying
to steal the love inside
It wants to steal

my natural beauty

People's fear and hatred
is dross absolutely
It marks like steal

upon the face
And scars it with intensity
sadness and anger lost grace
The lines on a face can

show the roads you've taken
Just remember to let
the small stuff be shaken

The big things will
pay a toll on you
Cannot hide it
cannot fake it

But what can you do
but lay back calmly take it
be the best revue

For no one will ever do you
better than you
Levitate your spirit
to a higher level in life

and believe all can be yours
My Grandma would tell me
"Pammy claim it and it's yours"

Allow no one to take pure love

A real sense of the amour
for if it is in you know true magic
You know what it does

Love is the only answer
I don't feel this is tragic
Practice with great reality

how to leave your troubles
two blocks back
there is no other way
to keep on track

I heard a stillness in the wind
enter my soul
and told me to hold on

and don't you let go
you have only one soul
Do not let the ugliness
ruin your world

Turn your face to the wind
and feel the peace
that surround your whirl

A Sense of Entitlement

It is really like going fishing
Daddy-o's advice You must have
the right bait "go to the right fishing
spot
at the right time and have patience"

Automatically looked at as a lower standard

but there was blood sweat tears shed all these years since the taking of this land
the Native Americans know this best and the others who are told they are ignorant
and Godless let me be your fake missionary

At best this was the start of all the mess
All is fair in war what about what is fair
in love it doesn't matter when there is a sense
of entitlement I am entitled to what is yours
and make it mine afterall God made it for our kind

When Rodney King was badly beaten
by the Police in the public street
It caused great horror, terror and sorrow
Within the African-American community
And those who are truly able to meet

the mind mass that we see how it was and how it is at one time in school we

were taught America is a melting pot
That one percent who has most the wealth
If you hold the purse string when everyone

is gone who will be there to remind you
why you accomplished your wealth
if no one is there to spend it what difference
does it make how much time and power you
put in this everyone else believe they will

take what is yours or they are kidding what
do they think you are ignorant if you believe
you will get what is mine in a false sense of
security remember a sense of entitlement is
taught from birth no one will meet their self worth

It brought back fears of yester years
Ugly crimes of ugly times
The Freedom Riders crime fighters
To fight this crime because America

had to raise its head and pay attention

Too many years of what its people
often did
Those with a sense of entitlement
Slave owners, people growers a
melting pot

high market for cheap labor, new
slaves
by prison wardens, prison yard
guards,
African-American overseers
In jail instead of cotton fields and
grape yields

producing license plates clothing
gadgets etcetera and financial gains
Like Mexicans Hmong poor whites
And other minority skins are also
trained

And African-American's, rioted
broken business
windows glass and looted with sticky
fingers,
Diapers, electronics, food and cash
did as this would equal the history of
the dead

In that situation the first thought
Are those who go after the big screen
TV
But the pampers and purified water
And special needs and medication
for the daughter how could this be

Well (taken back) could it be
survival
of the needy not just the greedy
Like Katrina when the government
flew overhead
There was an Asian woman who
was born
in a concentration camp on the
Pacific coast of America

And sent to Okalahoma where the
native Americans
Happened to travel from the east to
the west
Losing so many during the trail of
tears
In the past years of the Native
American
In Tulsa Oaklahoma colored
concentration camps

Caucasians assess and believe that
they are entitled
indeed of the benefits of the country
by their race
Because of their color and past
behavior to erase
And how humanity has handled a
situation as it
That doesn't fit what is truly going
on anymore
Has gone on for ages and pages

When the levees broke in Louisiana

And the government blew up one of the levees
There were people stranded for days
Stranded on roof tops who did not leave
Poor with no gas car or money

during the devastation couldn't reach out
to them it seem like the last days
People starving and with no clean water
milk for the babies, sick and the elderly
dead people floating in the water

and people who truly were left for dead
A sense of entitlement had nothing to lose
The others lingered around homeless
Waiting for their cries of outrage to be heard
There were news cameras flashing

And a young man dashed in and said
"Help wasn't being heard please step in!"
And with all the flashing cameras
And neglect and pandemonium lies
and the media showing those ties

who didn't care about those people

some were not the objective or the goal
Was it the last days? Of course this is
not cold a plane went over looked down
and then turned around looked profound

As the helicopters flew over
and they waved their hand to the sky
women and babies were left to cry
and die
on roof tops to die as the rescue helicopter
flew by what course has taught in time

A mother looked at a store
With broken windows and abandon
with water and glass food on the floor
some places finally am not saying that no one else
of color died or left behind

And those who were too old some from
times so old when for a change growth
But no matter how many years go by
there are certain people to change history and lie
but his story has let go of me

life puts me in reality we must want
to step out and help let go of those
feelings because all know right and
wrong
that choose to do people how they
long
and know we all are sisters and
brothers

a country divided shall truly fall
and now our backs are against the
wall
terrorism in the borders or an assault
on some just make sure you are not
the one
support human rights for everyone

through this a true sense what it
means to be
truly entitled too constitution rights
of equality
entitlements for the poor or rich
when not
redistributed may cost the country its
bareness
cost for more and greed an issue of
product

and demand remember a house
divided congress
cannot stand and refusing to
participate with
the leader of this land for some
people the

color of the hand that holds that pen
strike the fear of men who
understand

His study in life as civil rights
attorney affect
the thoughts to cure this land direct
so hard
there are group of men who cry
redistribution
of wealth is their scare tactic at hand
but it should tell you something
when you

President Obama at present day
the country by the
people was placed in his hand
it was so bad they wanted
real change fast he said "I'll get up

if supporters fight with me"
he knew he had enemies at hand
that would show their racism
before saving all the people they can
even if it means killing

their own to make a point
to man that cried change
get up and do you and get it
straight while this last
But before a man of color

can tell them anything in trouble and sit
like mules before they help him pass

a bill knowing their own need
healthcare and house shares

veterans gone gas soaring
food sky high no allibies
How long will people
help perpetuate the lies

Joyce Griffin

Love is the giver of light
And that giver of light loved you
A glimmer of light
was called away last Sunday
not just to make you dismal
not just to make you blue

But God knew of her pain and took
the burden away from you
I know you will miss her deeply
but another space she had to fill
Just keep your head to the sky
And know that God is real

Though today you will mourn
her passing
tomorrow your heart may seem torn
there is always a light side to every
story
and new life will often born
A dam of feelings may burst

And the flood gates hard to close

But in the night in solitude
her spirit and warmth comes close
A cloud burst full of falling tears
your mind clouded with all those years
Yet, behold MaMa's hands will hold
you tight

while the angel takes your fears
No more suffering remember what
we prayed
now you see that God's reality
are not just words that are said
God is a gardener, he plants his seeds
He waters, he cultivates, he prunes

and dust to heal our leaves
And when we have grown into our
beauty
he plucks us like a rose pretty
to spread around his mansion essence
intoxication never told
The only thing our death foretell

is that change must often come
So take a look inside your house
and make sure the cleanings done
He takes away a candle burned
and replace it with a new one
When he said "let there be light"

he meant it as the rule
It was time for Joyce to walk
and move amongst the stars
To climb that stairway to Heaven

God could see her heart
So be patient during this battle
a soldier of honor has been lain to rest

A Special Gift

as happy as a children holding
their first Easter egg basket
With an egg or candy inside
a mother is more elated holding
the children in her womb

bright colorful full of surprise and
wonder
and fragile when they are dropped
so diverse in character every egg
has its own flair and flaws
that requires great care
what special gift a mother bares

What a special gift a father shares
with the children that he raise or sire
by making sure they know their
name
and what it means to carry that
baton
sure somebody will accidently drop
one
but the next man who picks it up

Create a legacy of love for your
children

let him know that woman was
created
to be his helpmate if she's speaking
truth
good communication skills isn't
nagging
backbone and inspiration of any
man
loyalty and discipline is important

Valor

I am one for peace
But I definitely understand
that once there has
been a release of a beast
Boundaries are placed in front
of need and kind

I am proud for those who stand
to do the living in
Life take it head on
and are the lethal weapon
At times the battlegrounds
are not a field of play

You don't get to do it again
if you make a mistake
I understand the courage
the rights and the wrongs
I understand the loved ones
that are left alone

I am one for peace
because my need for a greater
Show of humanity to civilize
beyond man's mighty thrones
some day we will not be barbarians
some day we won't go there again

The Missionaries

Religion has been the mission
for those men and women
who do and do not know
our Lord, and savior, Jesus Christ
Jesus Je is in us as a child
in the church

I grew up hearing the name
Jehovah, Lord, Yahweh, Jesus
only I could claim my faith
That he would never leave me
especially when the world
would have me full of pain

"religious fanatic!", she just
talks about religion
and politics she shouts
she screams she cry things out
Being a true Christian

understanding the spiritualism
and the importance of forgiveness
I can love and forgive

those who inflict pain
but I must acknowledge it
bare the cross of it

have the right bait,
for a certain kind
of fish a specific line

in a certain place
at a certain time
My father tells me
to be patient
enjoy the love and beauty
nature

For years some people
couldn't read write or pray
It will take the great minds
sacrifices skills and
the love of all of us
if we bare the light

with a pure heart
omnipotent strong will
Muslims are terrorists
though the Quran reads
like refined poetry
Reading the King James Bible

fed me and put me
on my knees
Jewish people got
their money stolen

when attempting to pay
their way from the holocaust

the American Japanese
became home prisoners
for crimes of war
on a secret and a toss
The main war criminals
hide no more

It takes a coward
to not care about people
handing out numbers
not giving them
names and faces
This makes it easier

not to call it sociopath cases
Native Americans were savages
for protecting their
women and children
Heaven help us if
we don't come up with a plan

for those who always cry war
Could you imagine
if all were too lost to them
all their family members
in a giant blaze of gore
They could live knowing

they sold their family
for greed and personal ego

When the line is drawn
in the sand who will step forward?
It is a lesson of surrender
a lesson of great discord

in an era that it doesn't
fit anymore
we must become missionaries
those whom must become
healing leafs
green golden healing leafs

The Innauguration of President Barack Obama 2

This morning I cry for the blood
that run through my veins
the blood of ancestors
that built the house
that the first African-American

President of America
shall reign with a fine hand
of reincarnated spirit of all great
men
and my heart is flooded with
love democracy and joy

inspiring hope for the human being
acknowledging for the first time in
our country's history
that life is finally beginning

to see man is man

not determined by the color
of his skin
This morning I cry for the joy that
is a magnificent benevolent wonder
that keeps his promises

let grace be the glory
for all that maintained the hope
that in these univeral orders
vision has been maintained
through our prayers

we that wrestle to maintain
the ethics and morals
of righteous men transcended
Jesus Christ that I would
live to see this day in the flesh

a country still young in years
shout "free at last" my mind
is no longer enslaved and I can
see the victory at hand by
the wind so a new day that

all men are equal
abolished by a people
who on all sides of
the atrocity of this horror
will start to dwindle away

like a bad nightmare

the dream of Abraham Martin
and John and the unsung soldiers
of all flesh fighting for this day
The forefathers wrote

the United States Constitution
and the truth
that the human beings
that it has always been
the fact that all men

can now know freedom
because of the people
all men are free
not just the few who pretend
to be for all men can only

know this if his brother is free
this is a great day
I never heard a black man say
"I want to make another man my
slave"
I cry with pride and humility

but tomorrow will be another day
for the die hards in
this country will always contend
to have it their way
the land of genocide and slavery

but oh how sweet the victory
No, I am not a biggot
terrorist treasonist or a hater

I have a little Irish cream
in my coffee

Understand I love all of me
and all humanity
I have to petition
Everyone has a mission
And now the frozen moment

in time is over
I never seen a
President so disrespected
who put some of the best
people around him to

cradle a fragile country
that is falling like Babylon
For those of you who
remember the late great
Bob Marley

to pull us out of the last Republican
administations grind
The last President said you were
either for him or against him
there was no gray matter
Here is a President for bi-partisan

compromise or you kidding
the only thing they wish for is to dim
all the people's eyes we will follow
each other to the pit of hell
compromise
for what they entitled to bail

Dr. Martin Luther King

A splendid Man
Amen a man who understood
advocacy and ministry
equality and soliliquy

A spirit that lead civilization
to higher elevation
the majestic amethyst mountains
raising souls truly a man

given a master plan
He answered destiny
he answered his calling
some died crossing the ocean
floor with stories untold

yet history unfolds
millions and millions of Africans
died coming to America
to be living at this time in his story
the testimony of a strong people

that has planted root grown trees
and eat of its' fruit
who of us still hear you? Reverand
Dr. Marin Luther King, Jr.
You wield a might with your sword

more so in transformation
than here in the human flesh
thrown and gourd down by the bulls
whom fought with the mighty men

Omnipotent power showed the works

a miracle to get past the lash
women and children to stand
for their very existence
supernatural is in all things standing
in stillness he heard freedom

bells that ring in life all things
are reasoned for in all things
it does exist I raise my arms
to you and will hold you until
there is no reason

it is power in the word that makes
a man rise stand on his feet and take
risk
it is power in his movement that
determines
the strong from the weak in the
season
and march on even when all seems
to be lost

in your eyes you see nothing
but gain that never would have
came without
the knowledge of the pain and
the knowledge of that which was the
lost
I invoke unto you on this beloved
day

all your prayers to you as a martyr
whom prayed and laid even in
revealation
it was song from that same
mountain top
as truth that your death was a
conspiracy
ring and if this is wrong

Let the truth be known
because hatred will try to turn out
any light from
the voices of Georgia's freedom flop
and those who cried and prayed on

the battle field of life
as a butterfly is freed free me
because I know by the pain
still felt in my heart
we are close and yet still so far apart

we honor you this day
in your very special way
proud of who we are
where we come from
where we are going

The Rainbow Coalition

There is a rainbow coalition
and the colors are so beautiful
colors of our auras

cleansed is our countries pot of gold
found at the bottom of the rainbow

There are wonders
all around us and the fruit
we bite off are amethyst
egg plant parmesan with a kiss

emerald grapes juicy and sweet
citrine and green taste like salad
or a keylime pie twist
tourmaline lemons makes my
favorite
lemonade persuade me to drink it

carnelian and crystal quartz peaches
their power very strong beseeches
Heal the tummy the heart the psyche
these gems of wonder beauty and
power

2:22 Haunts Me

Explosive are my thoughts
as I lay here living in a place

a crawl space called fear
and I hope triggering

the memory of a certain year
will stear me

clear of repetitive

thoughts of someone

so dear confirmation
a situation

the clock's face showing me
digital 2:22 a.m.

A time when I was awaken
 in my youth

by a train so loud
vibrating the ground

it seem impossible
to hear a train

too far away as a recluse
When my mother's

youngest sister
had taken her own life

no longer could she take
the world's strife

swallowing almost
a 500 hundred

count bottle of aspirin
and no it wasn't for a cheap thrill

or a dose of high fashion
 she was hopeless

31

when she decided
to swallow the pills

words I remember
that flew from her lips

a few days before
watching her come to my

grandmother's house
In and out the front door

of her parent's house restless
she took her life

a couple of weeks
after her dead spouse

"People do not care anymore"
she said

"my husband lay dead
as a homeless man

who slept in a shed
his family claimed

him already dead"
Every time she left

her parent's home
it didn't matter that

she wasn't alone
for her it wasn't enough

that they could only
afford to care

at the moment for their own
They appealed to his family

but he was dead long ago
My emotions went out to her

but it wasn't enough
to keep her here

from the land of transformation
for those who are mentally tired

and forget about salvation
she called everyone's bluff

She kept smiling
for everyones sake

(hurt) confusion kept
calling her fate

Smiling reticent and aloof
was her choice of mask

she considerably used but
couldn't pass discernment

she wasn't telling the truth
when I wondered

if anyone could see it
the family considered

it my imagination and youth
That this message

would always linger
in my hard drive

and when I see the time
2:22

my recollection of the sound
a train when the horn blows

bring back my family's pain
still until this day

I wonder how the vibes
awakened me

that morning that day
that particular way

Now I only read
those numbers as an omen

and a showman
in a play we must turn

around and look
and stop pointing

the fingers
at the least of all men

to someone
they are as singers

sometimes doubt sticks
us by our own stingers

I will love my aunt
forever held like a

commitment ring
upon the finger that time

2:22
is my alarm ringer

Zero

I couldn't love you more
or less than I do right now I
am at absolute zero

Mask

(the Villain or the Gargoyle)
In this time of darkness
of the world

it is so easy to separate
the light from
the distraction of evil
At this time the
multi masks are being taken

off the flesh of cons
because there is no time
To play the game of hide
and go seek and if
I am unsuspecting and nice
you can take
any thing from me
If someone does not know you

then why do they look at you
with such disdain such hate
and contempt?
And that person has not
met you ever…not even
in Never Ever land?
The stench of ugliness

fill my nostrils and the
look of your face
burn my eyes as if shampoo
Pepper or Acid are waging war
to the point they ask for blindness
And our youth
act as if manners are a disease
and etiquette affects some of them

like a plague
My grandmother taught me

that a woman holds
the keys to the city
what she has between her legs
is worth more than rubies and pearls
Now they hand it out like flyers
and the price is so low

it's like a discount store
It is a house of desperation
they give it away like candy
Please someone tell me
there is a method
to the madness
tell me people are just scared
and they are hoping

to scare Villains off
and you are unable
to tell the difference
Rage….so many mobs
will contact each other over
the internet show up
at a particular spot and let
out their rage

But how many years
have the youth
been lied too?
Could this be the illness
behind Columbine
and other tragedies?
if you can't trust your teachers
your school counselors

your peers and your family
who can you trust?
Trust in God is on the dollar
bills then what?
but I cannot quit remembering
the words "You do not fit"
well I'll continue
to use my wit

than be a square peg
that fits in a round hole "smiling"
I am so happy
I lay on the deck
the passenger of a cruise ship
on the soft waves
of the deep blue sea

A Quest for Love

What is more important
than a quest for love
True lovers know
it has nothing to do
with color culture
cast or creed no
amount of money

It has nothing to do
with society's set of rules
or reason there are those
who believe it has
caused treason
ethics, morals, principles,

illusions and delusions

Conclusion:
The reality is that when
you love someone
there are no choices
to be made
the Heart cannot
help who it loves
when it comes to love

love makes the rules
for you are caught in
a quantum physical
moment of zen
thrown about like tiger
that has caught his prey
in his den

paradoxical intoxication
a ruthless
wind that somehow
skips over you
a false sense of love
when trust knows
no boundaries

emotions will sweep
you away
like dust in a tornado
and before you know it
there is no way out
unconditional love tells
you no matter what

even if it does not involve
me in the persons life
I am not the star of the show
yet I have another
part in that do we
make each other glow
thus grow yes

love thus is a splendid thing
when understood
the power if used good
as the love I would want to be
I would radther see
my love with whom he chose
than to be in a sad or bad

situation because of me
real love requires
true boundaries
sitting out sometimes
doesn't hurt it heals
it elevates one
to the higher hill

because I know I am
capable of loving me
therefore I am capable
and know how to love
another
I am not a vampire
to suck them of their energy

I can understand
the need of how love must

encompass someone else
the warmth it brings
into my self
to share that with
the opposite half of me

caress and hold
that heart carefully
it seems that when
we are least looking
for love
love seeks us out
just two wonderful people

that happen to trip and fall
into the arms of each other
was there ever a promise
that love would be easy?
not sleezy or cheezy
but somehow always is pleasing
love never have and

never will kill
people not the emotion
signed up for that deal
Respect and appreciation
it is a must
to be learned and earned

most of us know
it doesn't come easy
I just wish for a strong mate
that can stand and fight
have patience and grace

like a courageous soldier
be loyal for a relationship

be bolder
and perhaps love could
reshape the world
live and so will love
until the last breath
love until it is the last laugh
for rest a time to be heard

until you mumble
the last cherished
all honey sweet words
that are said
to me and apologize
for any emotional cries
or regrets afflicted by me

in my neglect and now I have
a quest for love I cannot forget
To have ever had the feeling of
love one can never forget
I would like to be cupid
if only for a moment
To be able to shoot an arrow bullseye

Dancing Heart

when I hear instruments
my spirit spreads its wings
as my cymbals ting,
ting-ting, ting

my vision is like an
osculate on my face

My heart dance
my vocals sings
body participating
to the music
my spirit brings
It will not allow

me to wait
as I anticipate sheer
joy so outrageous
the attitude in the room
is contagious
When I feel the notes

vibrate into my bones
and my mind is full blown
eyes into a trance
my feet prance the romance
and the spirit shone
is an alchemical stone

I am in the zone
a dimension all my own
belly dancing with undulations
the hip circles
Gyrations and rotations
leaving traces on those faces

looking hypnotized without insulting
my reputation
That is my Poetry to the dance

under any visualization
I cannot help but to move
under the circumstance

Music moves my soul
as light grows a plant
Depending on the sound
my rite of buoyancy and grace
the elegance of the sound
illuminates the beauty the elegance

so profound
A rhythmic walk down
lover's lane
as the dancing placate me
high amongst the stars
rhythm pulsate

silky smooth romance
But as a lover of the dance
knows there is no better chance
than the music that moves me
to that dangerous temptation
Not because it is bad

but my neck wants
to move rhythmatically
By the vibration
the poetry of the music
makes a dancing heart
Is spiritually moved

Running Waters

sweet and kind
smooth the things
that blows my mind
False thoughts are nightmares
everywhere that leads
us to ponder
if anyone cares

The roaring of the rapid flow
Sweet waters whisper very low
My reflection in the Lake
purify my essence
free my spirit
keep it whole

sanctified waters
cleanse me bold
make the mends
upon my rented robe
Run deep waters
through my bones
for we are all waters

some are calm
and some are rollng
and like the river flowing
coasting past the riverbanks
along life's way
we take a little
bit of sand with us

each and every wave

we take a little
bit of sand with us
each
time leaving the
changing shores
picking up multitudes of ever mores

to carry along and open doors
amours, repose, so sure
When we leave our mark
upon this lonesome quest
it is important to do our best
remember our job must
be well done

it does not matter
whether King or pawn
to know the time
when the waters are to stand still
to know the time
when the waters must roll on
when it is our moment

for our river to flow and rush into
the ocean positively in motion
those things we chose to learn
those lessons it seem we earned
are those the things
we have concerned along the day?
The world entwined in many way

what is the phase?
I ask myself is my misison blessed?
Has the sleeper been awakened?

Have I been my brother's
keeper, or did I sleep
the slumber wise?
We are running waters

Chronic Pain

A tear runs down my face
emotionally broken mind
unfocused
feeling like right now
life is a waste

choking on all the pain
that echoes in my brain
again and again
laughter gone
serious looks on my face

my nights are long dark
eyes puffy
my friend name Sleep
has lost my number
and is avoiding me

nightmares creep
when I fall asleep
constantly fighting
for my rights
to care for my disability

who shall I talk too?
Who wants to listen

to all I must do?
A life time of listening
and hearing

is gifted to few
when you lay on the couch
are you listening to them
do they hear and listen to you
My spine seems

to bend and bend
down to my end my dome ache
taking pain killers
that know me by name
this is insanity?

It isn't a game
I wouldn't wish it on
Any humanity
the torture is brutallity
as they easily tell me

knowing they would
want no one
to operate on their neck
with all the nerves
and muscles that twist curves

and the pain isn't gone
does it affect anyone?
You know if you treat them
the way you have me
Is your heart stone cold?

Please don't answer
let me hold on
to something in this
painful girdle
Chronic pain is cruel

venting is a coping tool
To utilize when tears are in the
wind
hoping to find my friend
if you locate Sleep
Tell Sleep to call me

come over
good Sleep do you know
how long it has been?
The treatment of humanity
You wake up in the morning

for a handy bus ride
and you get a person
who is empty inside
they do not understand
it took all that you have to give

to get yourself together
and pull yourself up stiff as steel
eyes watering from allergies
left eye is blurry
how much do they think

I can take?
Either I look awfuuly strong
or they are awfuly fake

Some of these dis- eases
could be ended

and I wouldn't be in
wait and offended
I wait for the medications
I have swallowed to hit me
before I get to the doctor

and the person at the desk
act as if she is aggravated
that you bothered her
now a pest to sign in
and she looks at you

as if you are trouble
the look is......
'I wish you'd drop dead
so you would be one less patient
to deal with tomorrow

where the person
who take your vitals
look at you
as if you're aware
that your blood pressure is high

It isn't going down
so when does your
blood pressure medicine
bring Sleep's friend
Feeling Better around

The doctor rights

for preauthorizations
that takes years
and much contemplation
the handy ride bus driver

makes it back
like the lotto
you may get a human being
or an uncaring jack...
I am scared to end up

completely still quadarpledgic
paraplegic if people
are this cold
that is worse than
growing old

the wickedness in those
who do not love in
the medical field
that must happen to heal
if I move my head wrong

and fall dead
not to mention
the other illnesses
I harbor within
I try to do what

the doctor says
and read and do what I can
then there are others
who would radther I sin
Then the doctor

41

writes a prescription
to help the pain
And the pharmacy
says the insurance
will fight this prescription

just the same as
I am trying to mentally
and physically
spiritually fighting for my life
there are those around

that want me
to give up the fight
why do I say this with such surety
because it has been
over 19 years

How could they
think and say I am fine
But I feel worse than ever
and I have people mad
because I had a good day

and I answer the door or
walk with a smile on my face
It is wicked I often wonder
what they would do in my place
I often wonder

what it would be like
if they took on my name
I wonder If they were me

would life be the same
would you trade places with me

Shape Shifter

If thoughts are things
I'd spread my wings
and rise like the Phoenix
from the ashes
build a civilization

that man couldn't
imagine nor vision
only the creator
the Greatfrandfather
of the Universe could fathom

I'd shape shift into
a hummingbird and make music
as beautiful as the harps
of an angels
I'd see the lyrics

in the rivers
I'd see the notes in the tree
and hear the voices of the
Archangels rejoicing
for the peace bestowed

upon the planet earth
I'd gaze the world
in my flight as the eagle

42

courageous
and attack my prey with claws

strong as a falcon
and destroy and uprising
of vile, evil, sadistic twisted
entities
that would be old enough

to rise against love and peace...
Shapeshifter
now I am the raven
the all seeing eye of the creator
sign amongst sign

hope of all hope
from the ancient of the
fifth dynasty Amon to Amen
one power one of hope
and dream one message

one of hope and dreams
one vision
men dare to dream
think dream know dream
hope dream imagination reality

And with the wisdom
of the great white owl
discern reality from illusion
while the world was sleeping
the sleeper awakened

never to sleep again
not by day nor by night
my huge white wings
would cover the sky
so bright I'd shift

into the moonlight
The soft touch of my feather
would brush away
any pain or displeasure
of the taste of poison

that wrestles with out wit
and blow away the ashes
and when I am the grass bird
I will hop from branch to branch
and skip from tree to tree

Nestle on my stomach
and be happy as can be
and say "thank you
Greathgrandfather
for making me"

Symphony

I hear a symphony
the symbals clash and fill my ears
yule tides it arranges
my spirit and the strings
drop my shoulders
I am one with the strings

after and a flash of light
and I see the most
bodacious creatures
I see the arms sweeping
slowly across its stem
and the leaves move

slowly side to side
as if it were a ballet
the drum richochets
throwing the pollen
up in the air as it float
down to the earth with love

and pollenate the flower world
the cello as mello as the
touch of a woman
with a quality resin like Honey
who knows her Venus mood
to exude as lovely a characters

as the horns with their heavenly
barrier
I hear love call my name
as the Symphony entertains
without knowing that it shed
my pain

Family

There are some moments
that are defining
when this is known

embrace it
when you embrace it
own it
as the acknowledgment
of this stability about

As a mother bear that will
fiercey protect her cubs
just find the excitement
emmersed in Water
I find zen
I am now at peace with myself
to move forward evolve
and become a better person

than I was yesterday and I
will become a greater person
tomorrow than I am today
knowing my true
pot of gold is love
Those I love and those
who love me
accompany me to enjoy

this enormous celebration
in the clouds
thunder and lightening
the fresh smell of rain
exuberant drops
as the beauteous tears look
for we are family
something that has power

over all existence

Being in the moment
brings happiness
Let no man thing or entity
trick you in believing
that there is not life
after death
because life no matter

what language spoken
or what quantum physical nature
 as explained by science
has proved the omnipotent

power does exist
all my pain stumbles
blunders taught endurance
patience to accept what is real

wonders and miracles
for God is the giver
all things I am convinced
I am humbled and amazed
at the tolerence
God has given to me
by not chance
with chance came lesson

you find yourself in my shoes
of a similar size and style
always remember
there is light after the darkness
and happiness is promised
I see it in visions
Though you may miss me

when I am gone

I will be on the other side
waiting when it is time
for you to come back
to your maker

when you think of my name
or a moment we shared
good or bad smile
for at the moment

I am a touch away
although you cannot see me
I am there
share share share
so that someone
will be with you
on the way out
share share share

The Sun Kissed Moon

The large pupil in the sky
who knows the truth do you or I

it hides the secret of our youth
and burns us up in hot pursuit

reflected by some absorbed by others
underneath it all we all are brothers

nature's topaz shining bright

entrusted souls of guiding light

the day moon glows by its illuminous
rays
accounted for another phase

Father and mother together as one
United souls for the new day's dawn

the opulent beauty the pearl in its
vision
the beryl which surpasses the world
in its wisdom

the march of eternity the December
of infinity
acknowledged by all born under the
trinity

The Tarot Reader

When my tower
came crumbling down
all my bricks lay
on the ground

the two of swords
came fast my way
and told me apprehensively
fast things coming to stay

and told me things
would stay the same

now the King of Cups
is upside down

is he possibly
playing around
the Queen of Pentacles
stands her Ground

the Fool moves by faith
for what he cannot see
just that hint
tells you be careful
sat love free

for only by faith
can I make the next move
but the High Priestess tells you
don't lose your cool

now the King of Pentacles
show you how
to rule command respect
in all he'll do

Caged Minds
and Lost Birds

Why cry about tomorrow
When you don't
understand yesterday
If all your beliefs
has been put in your head
by others brains

The brain never looked at
like a blank page
Who wrote the script
in the manner you act on
Surely it is fine acting

not the things that
fall from your mouth
But hate treachery
of cunningness
for the ants coming from

a teacher professing
to be the merciful
understanding the victim
teach caged birds
to think outside

Within the boundaries
of the cage
I had these beautiful
caged love birds

One night one bird Jet
fluttered his wings
wildly in the cage
I thought there were
merely feathers flying

But there was no
chirp or tweeting
When I went through
my head for what
had occurred

I walked passed the cage
several times that morning
Any other time
I would have fed them
waking upon a dime

Until finally
I looked into the cage
And ants was covering
its dead body
spirit released already

its mate was sitting
on top of him
quiet and strange
A band of ants
had a caravan

through their bars
like the best assassins
after a hard target
ate them alive because
they had no place to fly

Only if I had paid
more attention that night
I held the last love bird
in my hand
I did all I could do of

him and her that day
But it was too late
Before its dying breath
let out how I feel

for our feathered friends

I know it left a hole
in my heart
But what I truly
want to understand
how can humanity

do this to people
without criminal clout
We must stay human
we are not beast
And as a man told me

I have seen men who
treat their pets better than
they treat some women
tell women that they love
them and yet they

treat their dogs better
for he would never
put his hand on his dog
but put his hand on you
not put a cruel hand

an animal
And the woman
he claim to love her
beat her
without hesitation

and doubt the situation out of
your control

People held in cages
and locked doors
Because of their hate

for people of creed color
gender or the willingness
of people to speak the life
they have lived those caged birds

Johnnie

When Johnnie got his papers last
week
he thought he'd live his dreams
But the war time called him out of
life
now it wasn't what it seemed

I believe in truth and love
"my country's 'tis of thee"
as he shouted out in pain
"Why should I go fight a war
when there is nothing to gain?"

He started drinking heavily
in a land that was bizarre
Somehow it was little America
in the middle of the desert star

Out of the wind
came a caravan uncovered
from the ground
Land mines fill their road in

a space that once had buildings

Now metal shrouds and doubts
Horror was on Johnnies face
as he struggled with his past
He saw his favorite Super Bowl

game and heard Aunt Thelma's
crazy laugh
He saw mama with her Gucci
pocket book she asked him
for when he gasped
And Margie with her night gown
when

he came home on leave just past
Then on a horse so dark and grim
came death upon the shore
Johnnie looked to the right of him

and his friend was there no more
Death picked him up and slung him
past
the tank as the window blew
Shattered to pieces on the ground
was Sergeant Cain and Blue

Johnnie's anger now on his face his
wife would miss him at home
His children never to see their Dad
would cry when he is gone

Then Death turned upon his horse
and head Johnnie's way

He swallowed and took his last
breath
and wondered was it Judgment day
Now Johnnie's body was never found

and his dreams never known too
His wife heard "Taps" and took
a crisply fold flag and hated her
country soon
"He didn't ask to go" she said,

"He never would have left me
With two beautiful children we
prayed for
and a payment on our home"
But Johnnie no longer sleeps at night
when the guns go off in his head

"I'm sorry Johnnie I would have
went
if they'd asked me instead of you
But I was just your wife to them
with two of your kids and stuck on
you

Come darling now and rest with
me"
she tucks him under the sheet as she
weeps
He didn't know that his will was
strong
and he'd be going home
a courageous spirit roaming free.

The Seven Principles

There are seven continents
the seven churches
the seven religions who
hold the light of the
quantum physical aspect
of the seventh root race
seven days of creation

seven to discipline the self: truth
liberty freedom love
respect honor loyalty
seven deadly sins
sloth lust envy greed
gluttony pride wrath
seven main chakras

take a moment
and close your eyes
Now visualize being
on the beach
at midnight watching
the tides come
to shore and leave

back ocean roar
bio-rhythm
reading you by your flow
also with the ability
of teaching self control
seven is a lucky number
are you willing to let it roll

Why?

Why must we suffer?
it seems to be
a partner with pain
must there always
be sacrifice to
realize all we
have to gain

stand up within
the strength of
determination
for what we believe in
what we know deep
in our hearts

what is right
If we do not have the
a moral fortitutde
we could be no loyalty
for any price
accept the ethical compass

of those ships
that has crashed
slamming into
not fail to
remember history's
creations because

we are living them today
so we must
plant strength

in our garden
of determination
the advance of

common sense
for us to have
a better tomorrow
today we must
plant the seeds
of intelligence and

Get our heads
back into reality
Know that our voices
need to be heard
rid ourselves
of our sorrows

we are our best
advocates
we have democracy
for the first time in
history kept
aware of what

is taking place
and get to participate
people were paying
attention
I asked a PA
talking to me in the

doctor office one day
what he thought

about President
Barrak Obama's health
care plan he thought
it was a bad

Idea and it would
mess things up
for real it is
a borrible plan
and America
would pay for it

I asked him had
he read or seen
the health care
reform act did he know
anything about it?
He told me, ""no""

and to that
answer I'll rest
forcefully move
to do our best
those votes do count
they do make a difference

we must stand strong
in our vigilance
people died to
get these rights
let no one deceive you
of the fight

Commrades Men of War

I feel Horrible!
Who left the stars
to shine so bright?

The penetrating glass
cutting into
my eyeballs to
the sockets they call light?

Such strong fingers hands
clasped so tight
to catch a falling star
soldiers and civilians

dead bodies to the left of me
dead bodies to the right of me
All I hear from my country
is; fight! Fight! Fight!

And We are right!
Life is pricless
Now it's less than a penny
courage and strength

we have plenty
Men on reserve not so many
Or, a dollar maybe
two a day and how?

Many men on reserve again
we do not have so many
I met a young man who told me

he had served two tours

All his Senior class mates
from High School
that went with him had died
because his country men lied

all but two were fried
The young man is now playing
with thoughts of suicide
suicidal thoughts that hunt him

continuously at night
would let him be
and the shackles of guilt
saying,"why not me?"

Betrayl mean thoughts
intention is where the battle is false
At what price glory
At what cost the battle is lost?r

Hey H

someday the world
will listen too
the songs of nature
calling to awaken
us to our first state of being

the words will elevate
us out of a state
out of a state of misery

the things of thought
created from chaos

notes of distant birds
no longer enslaving
our movements unbinding
our souls losing our minds
defining the times
of a dark era

awakening the dawn
and seeking the sun
someday we will see
our purpose and
heed the tides
the rhythmic waves upon
the surface of the murky grave

Elizabeth

Awe struck as a child
by your acting ability
in "Whose Afraid of Virginia Wolf"

or "Cat on a Hot Tin Roof"
"Blue Velvet" "Your beauty"
in movies and your love

and tenacity
out shined the brightness
as your jewels

I know why they found

their way into your history
like the men

they were meant to be
You will truly be missed
you blazed like

a star in the sky
all conversation is in
those amethyst eyes

Walls Talk

On these walls
spattered on the paint
Are words that cut
to the deepest
core of my being

Now in my head
they are words
that are purposely ignored
I tried to turn out
the light on the wall
and permanently

forget that night
Forget to go to sleep
so I won't be able to peep
at the awaken to
the recording of the
layers of picture screens

Soaked Of terror
jealousy hate ruthlessness
and anger
The profane language
not knowing where
to lay and stay

Won't find its place
to go to sleep
But the nightmare
kept knocking softly
and then loudly to
Get the secrets out

Turn off the light
and press upon my feelings
By stealing what is more
priceless than rubies
diamonds and gold
He took my gifts

tried to steal my soul
And as the fierce
hands that rushed
upon my flesh
beat so cold
like a snake folds

Within these walls
is the picture of Satan
laying on the bed relaxed
Hands clasped arrogantly
behind his head

holding the back

of his head
With a wicked
look of control
the walls scream
looking at me
smiling as he's wishing

me dead
As a tornado of fists
searching for the best way
to make my body pay
Left inside with a criminal
to die if I didn't

resort to lies
How can a young woman
so bright get caught up in
In these walls
Lucifer penetrated me
he wanted

to dis-ease
as he pleased he!
Wanted to devastate me
leave me blind; so distracted
I could no longer see
crippled broken

into little bitty pieces
where he assumed cold

Share share share

share, share, share,
were the words
grandma kept saying
when I took an
acquaintance of mine
to the hospital
on a visit that wanted
to meet her

Grandma kept
saying these words
as the elders do of old
when they are born
spiritual teachers
The acquaintance
wanted to know why
she kept saying

those three words
"share share share"
I told her that
I would ask her
because my grandma
was dying
needing to be heard
So, I asked grandma

what she meant
by saying share
three times in a row
I pay attention to Omens
like the positions

as I see crows in
She stated,
"Pammy, last night
my friends
came to take me out
I put on my best clothes
because those who came
to get me were some kind
of sharp
were sharper than sharp

As we headed
out the door
I heard this voice
that came in my head,
it said, "turn around
and go back home
your children need
you instead"

She looked at me
and said, "share share share,
so that when you
are dying,
at least there will
be one person
there for you on
your way out"

When I told my
acquaintance the message
she begin crying
Every now and then
I remember those words

55

more importantly
I try to live them
The world is our family
and the children
on it are limitless
Share share share
so there will at least
be one person
there for you on the
way out

Men of War

Loud bombs drop
tut tut tut tut tut
my ears ring and pop
whether or not
on the guilty or rot
innocent hands

we were lied too
with all we had
to do a vote of congress
and the pentagon sprung
into action
upon the Iraqui people

with small
circumstantial evidence
plus reasonable doubt
Bush sent our military out
from amongst us they went
in with a crooked plan

rat a tat tat boom boom
fire plumes
loud screams broken dreams
never too be reached
promises breached
all about deceit

desires denied but at home
all the pride that wailed
up inside
some American's cried
kill them terrorist murderers
some confused deserters

awol because their spirit fail
from weapons of mass
destruction
a tall tale of private discussion
Soldiers came to fight
with all their might

said the young man
who lost all but one friend
and when he came home
he prayed for death
he felt alone
full of guilt and PTSD

gassing the tanks
turned into false victory
then came the negative call
what were we doing
there afterall
Civillian blood paint

the walls
back at home
a big funeral procession line
time after time the coffins
came home flags draped
over the bones

and those wounded and mangled
rolled home
those big camel spiders
hitched a ride to
escape gun fire
and again liars

sprayed them with pesticide
and innocent men and
women died
of cancer this time
no distraction
with go go dancers

there is a time
to laugh a time to cry
a time for hope
a time to die
but I know one thing
my eyes are opened wide

we need our military
home by our side
home grown terrorists
are on the rise
these men of war
with faulty pride

Metamorphosis

If death should find me
as I am running
let life kiss my lips
as passionately as the hope
I see in a baby's eyes

Let my spirit caress the lands
that I dream about
and let my offspring's
toes strongly hold the earth
all its' trust and wisdom

with out doubt
if I should go without
that last good-bye
only remember my smiles
for that is truly I

and when you smile
for whatever reason
may fate possess your face
with warm embrace
I shall rest with you always

My Antagonist

My Antagonist calls
me every day
those who love me

tried to warn me

but I didn't hear it
that way

I start traveling forward like
a jet my antagonist
would call me

with so many stories
excuses and bets
A hypocritic chaotic vicissitude

that wasn't so nice
forth put now my strife
glory is simply deploring

because it is actually boring
to wake up everyday
as you try to work

this way and that way
I looked in the eyes
of the stranger inside

the picture frame of thought
what part did I play
since I didn't want trouble

in my space like a mad
gypsy on fire the flames
get higher and higher

as she plays the violin
viviously and putting

limitations on desires

Look here comes
the antagonist finding
his way in my book

My Comet

Bright as the moon
shining like a diamond
lit up like a star
flash like a comet
you are close to my heart
your touch is like magic

your kiss is finesse
your smile is a dream
that surpass all the rest
my beautiful soul mate
for you I will wait
the one love in my life
my destiny my fate

Miracles

I do believe in miracles
I see them every day
As the world goes
flashing by

Time is but a phase

Open the heart to
the needy kind
And understand life
has no binds
In your heart you
hold his treasure
A stranger's love

is hard to measure
So give this day
and always share
And let the world know

that you care
The only thing
you're bound to find
Love is a miracle

to the awesome grind
A child is born
of mortal mind
And seeks potential

in the immortal line
The thoughts that child
must have had
When entering the earth

through Heaven's portal
Facing the fact
he isn't mortal
What if the waters never parted?

And in the beginning

there was no word
I wonder if miracles
still would have happened
The question is not absurd!

Sadomasochism

You stepped on his heart
putting out a smoldering cigarette
with the back of your spike heal

sadistic is your pleasure that suits
you
Put out your cigarette viciously and
There is sexual gratification what
jubilation

To your masochistic mate you are his
treasure
because she didn't want you to stop
take down her hair and pull it out

But her no rhythm understanding of
Quantum physics of time
creating a brutal kill not only in the
mind

I listened to her talk about
her never getting over you
and your wicked imitation of slicing

Without patience into your own flesh

She knew love and love knew her
not
and the circus she walked in

was not about love there was
a twist in the plot were not of civility
Schizophrenically watch her explode
The critical poignant beings

Mystic Brew

I had a mystic vision
of our love in slumber's deep
but Pain cut through my heart
now illusions often creep

they say when you truly love
you let that love go free
now I face the sad reality
that we may never be

if you only knew a love
like this again you will never see
but time takes its' toll on all
now you stand incomplete sad and
empty

like tunnel vision your picture wasn't
clear
now you often wonder who's holding
that lost dream near maybe next
time

you'll realize how lucky you really
are

when God blesses your life dearly
with one of his loving rising stars

Poetry

I will orchestrate my mind
to come into my genius
I do have knowledge of myself, Yes

I will use my mouth to
speak of truths and freedoms
it is an instrument of it self

I will take my dreams
and I will see the visions
these thoughts are the things

my lips they speak about
I will use my hands
to welcome

peace and tranquility
for only then will I truly
understand life

without it's doubts
I'll spread my wings
and soar higher

than the highest mountains

the Heavens shall sing
and bellow out sweet muse

Yet see the real upon
reflective fountain waters
a shallow deep within

view of mystic brew
within the lines
fishing the souls of doves

that rest upon
the morning's dew
let us all love

the rhythm and the rhyming
the Masala of the harps
so meek with eager timing

the brutal
symphony of the crashing blunders
yet still the echoes of amazing
wonders

HARK! The mighty trumpet
sounded
the battle in myself
to win this hasty joy

the art of showing grace
and the endless beauty
are in the lyrics
and the painted metaphors

There is a Draft in Here

How is a person
capable of ripping off
anothers heart
and dare not to give it back?

War, or the mind set
can become unforseeable
before engaging the people
must honestly search themselves
and know why they are doing so?

War in the spiritual sense
is awesome within itself
all wars began with these two
before the physical war

But to ask of another soul
something that you cannot
bare to do yourself
Why? If thievery and lies
are the reason for war

why do those who vote
to send children to war
do not send their sons
and daughters as the sacrifice

for the spoils of war
and the loss of civilian
casualties on the battlefield?
Are not all equal as
it is written in the constitution?

What war can be won from
a draft of or for the
sake of livelihood?
I have not seen or

heard of any war
when the spirit is not
given to the will
to force men and women
to go into a war

that has asked the greatest
one of them
just surrender over
the children

for a maybe
not a for sure cause
Not from greed fear
or destruction terror
to see who has the biggest toys

that makes all the noise
we are watching it take us back
to a time of progression
when the world becomes

so unstable that it is
thrown off its balance
it only takes a feather
to tip it over
if mankind doesn't

understand
the importance of how
everything affects another
as united nations

the ultimate goal
should be world order
so that there might be peace
that commands a great leader
with intelligence strength

and common sense
and the rationalization
that all leaders should be thinking
like the five civilized tribes

civilization before the prophecy
so that there can be
the purging of mistakes
that there are those who
will not want to admit

what greed and tyrany is not
a man a slave
when their freedom is taken
away without consent

What man would be a coward
for a just war?
Fear exist that is how
we all gain courage
but I believe if you can

send children to war
No warrior's health care?
Is that a question
when there is loss of

life limb mind life?
I just say life should be
more meaningful
for if it is not
for those who say

we want more
I must have
if I can take
then I can take

whatever is yours
and make it mine
when in reality is it never
ours anyway
why is not the wealthy men

or the poor men not happy?
It is drafty over hear
close the windows
and give me a warm blanket
thank you the suffering

the pain and the anguish
of an aging humanity
in a world so technologically
advanced

but humanity is losing
all its ethics
morals manners
a sense of empathy
we shall bury our roots

into the ground
but what tree has
sprung forward?
Is it the tree of life?

We are experiencing
the tree of good and evil?
if I do not speak out now
Might I speak the truth
to myself if no one else?

when there is a future
for humanity that should know
the suicidal of its own nature
the lust for violence

the quest for power
and with power
comes a great responsibility
may I enlighten your hearts
there inside your secret chamber

there is any love
and truth is not a stranger
what happened to honor?
when did ego

and this is where I say by
to an old friend
for I have looked death
in the face so many times
I know that he will be coming

for me again one day
and on that day of my ascension
let me not doubt
let the invocation of these words

be as powerful as the need
for the end of a war
arrogance triumph runneth
over with integrity
a strong mind gives all good troops
honor

Magic

Love is magic
magic is love
Do not watch the sleight hand
hidden by the white glove

Illusion is another word for deceit
trickery
Magic it makes your whole life
complete

Watch him pull the rabbit out of the
hat

Imagine the lovely lady without her
fat

Redundant is nothing but overused
words
In the true wisdom you'll find that
these words must be heard

true love is the answer to all your life
wishes
Now close your eyes and take three
soft wet kisses

Magic just believe in love and the
wish is yours
keep your eyes on the hand in the
glove

The Innauguration of President Barack Obama

This morning I cry for the blood
that run through my veins
the blood of ancestors that
built the house
that the first African-American

President of America, shall reign
with a fine hand
of reincarnated spirit of all great
men
and my heart is flooded with love

democracy and joy

inspiring hope for the human being
acknowledging for the first time
in our country's history
that life is finally beginning
too see man is man

not determined by the color
of his skin
This morning I cry for
the joy that God
is a magnificent benevolent wonder

that keeps his promises let grace
be the glory for all that maintained
the hope; that in these univeral
orders
vision has been mintained
and through our prayers

we that wrestle to maintain the
ethics and morals
of righteous men transcended
by the blood of our lord and savior
Jesus Christ, that I would live
to see this day in the flesh

a country still young in years
shout "free at last" my mind
is no longer enslaved and
I can see the victory at hand by
the wind so a new day that slavery

is finally about to be

abolished by a people whom on all
sides of the atrocity of this horror
will start to dwindle away like
a bad nightmare and the
dream of Abraham Martin and
John
and the unsung soldiers

of all flesh fighting
for this day that the slave
forefathers wrote the
United States Constitution, and the
truth
that the human beings that it has
always been the fact that

all men can only know freedom
if all men are free
not just the few who pretend to be
but cannot be for all
men are free not just the few
who pretend to be but cannot be

for all men can only know this
if his brother is free
this is a great day and I cry
with pride and humility
but tomorrow will be another day
for the die hards in this counry

will always contend to have

it their way
the land of genocide and slavery
but oh how sweet the victory

written during the innaugeration

When A Mother Loves

she experience in her heart chamber
her children's jubilation
She dreams and catch as
a dream catcher holding the good
letting go of the bad
worrying about our children
can make us mentally mad
We want all the visions
they need fulfilled what they
have and what they had

But what about the children
that never see the other side
the ones a mother can't talk about
but in the closed she hides
Every now and then over time
they come back in our minds
and let us know there is nothing
we can do but try and leave
those thoughts behind

The pain is in my heart
and it won't go away
the man told her just run away
and you can still be saved

She prayed upon the table that God
would take her life too
But when she came awake still here
she cried and wished
for doom

Feather Strokes

I sit in this chair feeling
the feather strokes of a whirlwind
that raise my breast into
the want of your sensuous lips

My groin yearn with passion
guarded by restraint needing to feel
good

you are that one that awakened my
senses
the taste of love
has not touched my skin for a while
I can only imagine what it would
be like

your eyes they speak volumes to a
fiend
one day your flesh will touch my
flesh

and you will ask yourself what took
so long
for this is body poetry of a mad
woman

Wanting feather strokes of a world
wind too…..

The Trumpet

My mind blown
like a trumpet Loud!
sharp schematic proud
voiced opinions

over the years stored
like the creation
movement of clouds
sweeping the sky

tying to erase your name
frog cheeks
flapping in the breeze
did you recognize

that with great ease
you have the capability
of driving me insane
if I let you continue

to do your thing
I better watch you lover
teacher, brother,
sister, clergy, other

the choice of character
you have chose to play
sometimes clever

and shrewed

sometimes silly and rude
"You bare watching"
said the tired old man
dressed in his wisdom

mind moving
the information
he has taken into him
like a furious game of

badmitton or a tenacious
game of chess
just to tame
this distorted view

you have brought
about wanting to change
the rainbow hue
for you are like a future

full of great hope
and loving gain
Mind blown
like a loud trumpet

clouds the judgment
drop the rain
cleanse the environment
as the thoughts bounce

around like a large toad
the purple of the rainbow

burst through the clouds
with lightening and thunder

moved my mind
forward down the road
Loud noise can
become a distraction

or a song in the grand
scheme of things

Zero equals Love

The circle O is all we know
what we need know

if we are not to go down below
the magic that glows with double O

that is not a NO
we need it to grow

in all that we know
especially between us

one day we will show
Who possess the circle O

Ancestors

As I am on my way
to a tribal meeting an

ill thoughts fleeting
as my intuition
is telling me I am not
paying attention

to my often vision of being
tortured
And as the thought
entered my mind
I was jumped from behind
Then without my permission
from the bushes

came the man
that I once knew
as a friend
but knew
one day he'd be my end
My eyes huge
this new enemy

eyes of blue
took me to a spot
where men of royalty
and common lot
were being chained
about our necks
wrists and ankles

shackled strange language spoken
as we attempted
shouting some necks broken
by the viciousness
of the slave makers

whom captured us
with psychopathic insanity

As I attempted to struggle
I felt a blow to my head
and my knees buckled
When I opened
my eyes again
I no longer felt the wind
upon my sweaty skin

and my clothing
had been taken
my confidence was shaken
and the smell of fear
the stench of sickness
and rotting flesh
rats and dung had overcome

the memory of frankincense
and myrrh
life as I had known it
now would only be a blur
Packed in a wooden
can like sardines for months
some of us were thrown off

others jumped
when they could find a way
all around me the stench
of death
the smell coming from
myself began the proces
of becoming the beast of burden

angry as a man
women and children
I watched beat by
these strange hands
to throw up
what little slop
fed to keep us alive

When the docked ship
what new world was this?
Our new homeland
There were many
who didn't make it
I hope the generations
that last intake this thought

Meditate good and long:
Ancestors
As we made
the auction block treated
less than animals
in this twisted plot
as we were sold

to people who conspired
with other countries in the world
with the same desires
capitalistic means
Who knew we would
be put in the midst of
aquisition of a land

Aquisition of men
building these grand

buildings and institutions
built by our backs
and hands
was the plan
back to the auction

as a woman took
center stage
because she didn't
understand their ways
she was slapped
and pushed aside
she knew by now

not to show any pride
or these kidnappers
would kill her and the baby inside
right where she lay
Next came another woman
and the bidder
felt all on her

as he continued and opened
her mouth like a horse
and spread her legs with force
BAM! Sold!
name changed from
Zewdi to Mary
and her Owner's name Jones

You see he kept her for a breeder
feeling he spent a bit much
but with himself and a male buck

he can make him
a litter it's cheaper
so the wife can't be bitter
when he lay with her at night

see if a slave woman marry
her husband cannot put up a fight
My ancestor's say constantly
there is all kind of slavery
Don't turn your eyes
because in this day
anyone can cry

for their little girls boys
women and (sigh)
Ancestor's die and help
on the other side
and when you see them again
tell them how your life began
I have never heard a African-
American
Want to see any man in slavery

Gardener's Shears

One that which is real
comes from within
we as women share
not our real sins

we don't talk about
our real troubles
or how we overcome

instead we worry about

the next person said
and beat on broken drums
don't you know the phoenix
will only rise from the ashes?

These earthy things
and material panache's
fly by things
as if they had wings

our mistakes are the thorns
from which we grow the most
A gardener watches his beautiful
rose bush naturally grow

but when he see
something going wrong
a branch growing crooked
aphids on the sweet petals

he dusts he prunes
he fertilizes he nurtures
and grooms it until it blooms
he love it consistently

as it continues to grow
in the way it is trained to do so
and such is a beautiful
woman should be

so lovely treated

lovelier than the rose
with so much love
and life in her

spread about the path as she goes
her innocence her longing
for some tender love and care
as the persistent need
of some gardener's shears

The Gemini

I Am Gem in Eye of God!
I affirm my hominid
Slayer of the zodiac
Thoth rules this entity
by mercurial strength
the brilliance of Simeon

and Levi Guards the gate
influence me
taking that which allows
me to arise to my best
I am tested by the unrest of chaos
my obligation too extreme

regardless of request
that no matter
what part of the celestial pie
we are from
we all need to balance our work
until the job is done

The Unicorn

We are at the twilight
of a new begining
of an old ending

Time evolution that sparks
the revolution has brought
us to this quantum moment

building a new kingdom
promised before
the measurement of kind

What shall we bring
to the architect's table?
A city beautiful Zion

the lamb guarded by the lion
A peace once known
to man is known again

Human new creation
was put in his hand
Was that not the plan?

Or do we understand
we are at the birth
of a four square city

and there will always be a unicorn
Now Gabriel blow your horn
they have all been
warned

Zero equals Love

The circle O is all
we need know
if we are not to go
down below

it is the magic that glows
with the double O
that is not a NO
we need it to grow

in all that we know
especially between us
one day you will show
you possess the circle O

Dr. Martin Luther King

A splendid Man
Amen
a man who understood
advocacy and ministry
equality and soliliquy
A spirit that lead civilization
to higher elevation

the majestic amethyst mountains
raising souls truly
a man with a plan
He answered destiny
he answered his calling
A minister and civil rights leader

Africans died crossing

the ocean floor with stories
untold yet history unfolds
millions and millions
died coming to America
to be living at this time
in his story
the testimony of a strong people

that has planted root
grown trees and eat of its' fruit
Who of us still hear you?
Reverand, Dr. Marin Luther King,
Jr.
You wield a might with your sword
more so in transformation
than here in the human flesh

thrown and gourd down by the bulls
whom fought with the mighty men
Omnipotent power showed the works
a miracle to get past the lash
women and children to stand
for their very existence
supernatural is in all things
standing in stillness he heard
freedom bells that ring

in life all things are reasoned
for in all things God does exist
I raise my arms to you
and will hold you until
there is no reason

it is power in the word
that makes a man rise

stand on his feet and take risk
it is power in his movement
that determines
the strong from the weak
in this season
march on even when all
seems to be lost

in your eyes you seen
nothing but gain
that never would have came
without the knowledge of the pain
and the knowledge
of that which was the lost
I invoke you on this beloved day

all your prayers to you
as a martyr whom prayed
and laid even in revealation
it was song from that same
mountain top
as truth that your death
a conspiracy ring and if this is wrong
Let the truth be known

because hatred will try
to turn out any light
from the voices of Georgia's
freedom top
and those who cried and prayed
on the battle field of life

as a butterfly is freed

free me because I know
by the pain still felt in my heart
we are close and yet still
so far apart
we honor you this day
in your very special way
proud of who we are

where we come from
where we are going
of thee I sing
let freedom ring

Alva

Is a Powerful woman indeed
is a mother who teaches
the capability to do things your way
by example you can think outside
the box
and be careful where you play

To learn to be your own person
not care what others say
if you maintain this thought
learn character is not taught
and the status quo will work the
same

To have a want to give your best
believe in Omnipotent eternal bliss

to walk the road with blinders on
compete with self no one else
not afraid to be alone

She claim her throne
a woman who teaches you this
is a powerful mother indeed!
To keep tradition
when uncouth is cool and stay

hip by staying within the rules
when it comes to cooking food
an alchemist with intelligence
with a twist love a definite
ingredient

when it comes to the recipes she use
You are the best walking cookbook
you taught me it isn't the recipe
its in the cook
A woman of great stature

determination and flair
Has become everybody's mother
whom ever came
in contact of her care
bold gorgeous comforting

witty and cleaver
wisdom with her smarts
the woman
whom used her special talents
to become the Queen of hearts

Stoic in her aura
elegant in her poise
whom taught me
to take aging gracefully
and when nonsense knocks

upon my door I kill the noise

Saint Michael

(Woo lete Miskal)
the daughter of Saint Michael
greatest hero of the longest war
of all times that is the one
between good and evil
the Arch Angels and his

legions of Angels
shall carry the light
and the sickle to bury
in the souless demons
who won't give up the fight

Beware of Ghost and Goblins

Beware of the Ghost and Goblins
Those entities seen and unseen
that move along in the shadows
those who like to plague your life
and destroy your world with
kryptonite

Those unawares that came here
to steal your dreams turn them
into nightmares and burn you
with their eyes and smile
as you scream with terror

brought on by the fiends
These sneaky beings that pretend
to be your partner or your friend
unawares that have no cares
of ruining life and creating despair

Be careful of these creatures
they may get you caught up in the
grind
Beware of the Ghost and Ghoblins
those that wear mask to accomplish
their task to sneak up from behind

These putrid creatures if you look
closely they have no features
Who are these creatures
these entities that seek to destroy
the privedge of being a human
creature

Maintain in your head
that in spirit they are dead
and be careful of their deeds
the dread they weave
laughing as you bleed

dangerous clowns looking about for
others who are like them

putting people out on the limb
the end of mankind is fine with
them
keep your third eye open and clear

The Wheels on the Bus
Go Around 2

Why strange when a little colored
girl
born into a mixed up world
took a ride on a yellow bus
with little white kids desegregation
They yelled out screamed and
hollered
and kept up a fuss crying

"Nigger, Spear Chucker
go back to Africa! porch Monkey!"
I said," what?" in amazement
The bus driver was invisible
as I sat on the back seat of the bus
Is this why as a country we wade in
muck?
The wheels on the bus go around
and round
the wheels on the bus go around

Where is class manners ethics morals
obviously not in this middle class
horror
Here I was traveling with honor
students

I've known gangsters to be more
prudent
it is an essence of that which exist
and access to the best education
intelligence and finance wasn't their
representation at ten what a
realization

The wheels on the bus go around
and round
the wheels on the bus go around
There were two children
who road on that bus
Robert and Holly sibblings
who took up the fuss
"Leave her alone
she has done nothing to you

You need to shut up
before you are black and blue"
the wheels on the bus go around and
round
the wheels on the bus go around
I was astounded as a child I knew
coloreds
were killed but not colored children
too
that was the deception our family
did not
want us to see I understand it felt so
ugly

the colored students were clenching
their teeth

You would think the colored
children
would have found me astute instead
I was called oreo cookie lilly white
wanna be
The wheels on the bus go around
and round
the wheels on the bus go around
No one was there to protect me
I didn't say a word to my family

until many years had gone by
did I recognize I was too afraid to
cry
As the year went by and my race
was put aside
I had one of my best school years
of my life
The wheels on the bus go around
and round
the wheels on the bus go around

I was not able to take this for
granted
but it is not usually a bouquet of
roses
What caused all this furociousness
It was a time of civil rights
sense of entitlement
has brouht about,
Did the stealing
and selling and trading of slaves

Being released out of a criminal act

and when the country
civilization has caught up with fact
the wheels on the bus go round
and around the wheels on the bus go
around
what human would have it like that
generations been taught to hate
and the KKK profess to never go
away

like the confederate flag
will not stop it will stay
Hate crimes are still carried out
thats what happen
That has turned this
country on its' butt
These were the students
of the first gait program

I Q tested and the break
in segragation
this is what fell out
Come out
the student is clenching their teeth
You would think the colored
children
would have found me astute
instead I was an oreo cookie

a lilly white wanna be
the wheels on the bus go a round
and around the wheels on the bus
goes around
disgust, what made you

as a man
cheking grocries at the
check out stand

call me boy and accused
me and my cousin
of destroying the display of toys
the salesman knew
the white children did it
he was playing with them too
my pants flowered
my pig tails long

and raised to be respectful
in a place that was crazy wrong
what monster were you
and are you still living
or are you gone?
who are you to tell
women of color what
we aren't like and who

we really are
What we should look like
what we are like
what we love about ourselves
any others oh well
because we were not
Barbie because of our skin
I've been told mine

is really beautiful
you thought you

could scar me
well good luck
you only taught us that
your men lied aloud
when Willie Lynch taught torture
to a messed up ctowd

because you hid beneath the sheets
Conviction to stand
as your minds are lost
then I could understand
what one fifth of an animal
was the excuse
what it was all about
money capitalism control and abuse

laying right by your head
more deadly than you are
the venomous lips of
a blue eyed woman
there as you lied died
and cried rape
you made it bad for those
who are not like the kid

who called wolf
and told him that you cared
like you were on a date
money is your pleasure
tell her to check your underwear
who have you been lying too
her him me or you
anyone anwhere

Awww genocide against my people
had to run and hide
did you bury the bones
under the rubble of the city of Gould
calling us savages
as the ancestors were saving their
babbits
and less than people as you went into
marraiges
church hands clench under the
steeple

and told all that God thought us as
evil and cursed people born to be
slaves
or put into the grave
if this was our lesson
then we must look for a blessing
marrying and yet judging
all cultural people
but if karma has its way

I wouldn't want no one who has
done evil
to experience that betraying lose your
hate
before it is too late

your children are not the same
and as they change
because your cruelty comes back
hasn't changed

as insane as it always have been

so now rewrite history
we must make it sound pretty
to what you really change self poison
say they are not to blame
But if fathers are teaching their sons
how long will humanity
waste its time

the universe has changed
and nothing remains the same
men of color must find their brain
so you will stop nailing them
to the same old game
around racism
running after your women
that you pimp when catching them
slipping

stop and lets turn this environment
around racism power is in the people
that is democracy
Power is meant for the man with
wisdom
intellience and common sense
The yellow bus and the grocery store
and many more
because the wheels on the bus go
around and round
the wheels on the bus go around

Greed

This day of January 19, 2011
Is one of reflection
on our financial situation.

One of the beautiful attributes
about freedom Is that we have
the right to make as much money

as we like in this Capitalistic
country
The concept reminds me of two
children sharing a bed

then having a tug of war
over the comforter that shields
them from the ruthless cold.

The comforter is too small
if they continue to fight it will tear
Eventually the more assertive

determined, aggressive, greedy
but most of all needy child do not see

that if he doesn't stop and assess
the situation from a different view

I am sure he will get more relaxation
He will rest better because he does

not have to watch his back
because the other child is warm too

He only had not to be over zealous
in the competition of the deed

But what I need to know is when
the greedy know the limitation of
greed

The child has the adoration
respect and kindness for his act

If the child is left alone
because the other child gets sick

or dies from cold who will he talk
too
where will he spend his money

what worth is his money if he is all
alone
with no one around to spend the
money grown

Simple Minds

I do not deal
with simple minds
simply because
they aren't my kind

their way of thinking
runs a muck
their stupid moves
they call bad luck

80

I don't deal
with simple minds
because their brain
waves are hard to find

they stumble about
scratch their heads
if they do not look up
they'll soon be dead

I do not deal
with simple minds
they always end up
in irrational binds

they always listen
to simple folk and then
become angry when
made the butt of jokes

simple minds try to find
what all self thinkers
leave behind
they eat filth drink nasty wine

good things tend
to hit the grind
simple minds
in simple times

the bottom line
in these truths we'll find
whether it be a lawyer
doctor, chief, or teacher

butcher, cake maker
do not deal with
the sensational fakers
take exception

take the time
before you deal
with simple minds

Temple

My body is my temple
unique as the spirit it holds
it cradles my mind
when insinct it will find
an inner peace

It swallows my lover
in the pit of its ecstacy
It endures the harsh
elements and ageless time
like a courageous soldier
My body it represents me

Tesfaye (Hope)

Don't give up hope
when chips are down
no one is around
don't give up hope

when things are bad

s.o.s. so sad
don't give up hope

when people are vicious
and being malicious
the biggest
con is on them
by their own actions
they have been bad
don't give up hope

born a in a world
that is twisted
you seem invisible
and someone has done
the unforgiveable
don't give up hope

when there you have a mission
they are clouding your vision
don't give up hope

dig deep within
when you have none
and you give all
don't give up hope

when you give
all you've got
in return you get heat back
don't give up hope

and when it seems
what is not

when all is sad and done
and you're the one
who has won
keep holding hope

the haters and perpertrater's
would toss you in the pit
of huge snakes
or alligators
don't give up hope

you see when it's all
said and done
and you are number one
remember life's stories
and all of its glory
all you have is hope

do not put it down
allowing bullying tactics
bad manners to spare
Yelling terrible threats
or physical battering
keeps you from chattering
don't give up hope
there are people who care

That Woman

I am that woman
a lady by right
True love is the
creator of day

and night

My bare feet
touch the earth
and all that is in it
I humbly bow
to absolute sweetness

skin blazing eyes
shining as the stars
are all around me
when the Lion
enters the room

I grab him by his tight
mango colored lips
with my third eye
piercing into his core silence
In his head he heard

me ask, "Are you my keeper?"
And the answer in his mind
Yes! Loud and very bold
That woman is in the core
of his soul

I Want A Man

I want a man to love me
Not think to control me
but he know that he
has my heart in his hand

He knows not to crush it
for it is as fragile
as the wing of a butterfly
But strong in knowledge

It is not a weakness
for either of us to cry
I want a man to crave me
ravishly dance with me

in our passion as he could
do it with no other
He feels what he needs
knows what he wants

I need a man to trust me
unselfishly not cheat
when he lacks integrity
and host insecurity

Be void of discipline
that strengthens the heart
Allowing "we" to grow as one
Not telling me when to go

or when to come
He doesn't operate
on the "down low"
Arouse me

with your sensibilities
let your tongue say
the proper words
you need a woman?

Soul mate

Bright as the moon
shining like a star
flash like a comet
you are close to my heart

your touch is like magic
your kisses finesse,
your smile is a dream
that surpass all the rest

my beautiful soulmate
for you I will wait
the one love in my life
my destiny my fate

Seminole/Cherokee

My roots are deep
toes long stretching
reaching into the soil
sound howling nature calling

in the large forest is the old
tree as my ancestors speak
Mother earth has a hold on me
under the highest mountain

ocean steep toes reaching
into the ground sound howling
Over the river bed
I listen stratosphere whispering

Whoooooooooohh calling
my ancestors talking
At one time the wind
could talk over my head

Hear your heart beat
instinct with nature
Boom-boom
at one with the beat

of the drum
Boom-boom
We all wait
for the transformation

We have always been
one with the land
there is much grace
in every bit of sand

speak I send the crows
the great white owl
They have been following

Don't Sip the Yak!

The drink is too heavy
to pour it back
remember these words

Don't sip the yak
Now those from old school
Know that yakity yak

meant you're not saying
anything said is worth
taking back

Wanting your mind
to take all of the deadly
Poison in cup

like the incident
in Guyana
Once you drink

it's too late
for I don't want
to sip that drink

Watching some
of the daily news
Make you wonder

what happened
to Walter Cronkite

But mostly
commentary goons
Lying as they

are dying inside
hoping to get the facts
without tarot or runes

Keep your intelligence
and faith get way
from word wasters soon

You can listen
to the conversation
It should spark

the intelligence to thinking
But if it is toxic
don't take it in

It will vex your spirit
tense pain in your head
and do not forget to blink

It may be the words
some are slang
it might sound wacky

Others might say
even tacky
what I am saying

Just remember
don't sip on the yak!
Get your mind back

Everyday we listen
to the news
We learn

who is at war
maybe why we are there
Maybe they will come here

statistics and public
conversations about politics

How many are making it

through a dying
injured economy
sacrifices of our families

Soldiers when
they come home
there will be thoughts

everything and every war
every political behavior
every civil right ignored

every disabilities act
every soldier whose loved
one was whacked

Don't sip on the yak
Every person needs
healthcare the elderly

every single parent
whether the war
was a just war or not

the mere fact
this man or woman
put their life on the line

to get where we have got
sacrifice them
for a while or forever

There were programs
set up of trusts
to be there when

we turn a certain age
O.k. some things
were not done right

they were not honest
are we doing what it takes
a lot more than the imagination

how horrible things
can really be
Just don't sip the yak

Herbs

Genesis 1:29 And God said
"behold I have given you
every herb baring seed
which is upon the face
of all earth and
every tree in the which
is the fruit of a seed
yielding tree; to you
eat shall be meat"

In America herbs are to
eat on meat and drink as teas
All these herbs are good indeed
you have herbs that help with fever

like feverfew
marjoram that helps with colds

mint that helps unplug your nose
and hisbiscus flowers that lower
blood pressure and the taste is a
pleaser and rue is a treasure to take
away headaches
and handle money matters

Medicinal Marijuana does many
things from
headaches to back aches to bad sight
and
lack of sleep
When it is hard for one
to eat marijuana
gives you truly the munchies
I say these things because
they are all true
ask the cancer patient
the muscular sclerosis
anxiety depression and spinal stenosis
too

we must look at medicine
for every need
and different types of
patients prefer different
types of needs
Whether it is western medicine
or eastern medicine like everything
else in life

the truth must be known so we can
make
proper choices for our life
we live in a democracy and we have
given our
vote and if we have to vote again it
won't change
what is known
That Holistic medicine is just
as important and strong
As laboratory medicine and
a lot safer than some
there are herbs that cause you
to urine and there are . . . . . .

El Munstruo

Why does the market media
some parents and adults market
children with padded bras

make up as if children are flawed
and fake butts and big hair false eye
lashes to bat everywhere
what if the pervert don't care
and if he's a mass murderer
there will be little pieces every

where they are so tuff with their
other stuff
and they look horid when you
lift the veil

and know how many children
are living hell

from pedofiles under the disguize
of other things
without the inticement of the
additives to those women
here and yet they are displeased
with over seas with veils down to

their knees are victims of male
dominance how does these
countries teach boys and men
how to keep their pants
do not just drop them under
any circumstance

women very beautiful and adorn
themselves elegantly
they are in bondage ask
a woman in pain
does she want
beauty or a brain

that thinks for itself
well it is called pimping
and pandering and creepy sneaky
handling of our babies and
please stop all the noise
now here you are for our little boys
el Munstruo let go you are just a
…....

No One Can Do You

Lord take away this
feeling inside
Something in life is trying
to steal the love inside
It wants to steal
my natural beauty
People's fear and hatred
is dross absolute

It marks like steal
upon the face
And scars it with intensity
sadness and anger lost grace
The lines on a face
can show the roads
you've taken

Just remember to let
the small stuff be shaken
The big things will play
a toll on you
Cannot hide it
cannot fake it
But what can you do is

lay back calmly and
be the best revue
For no one will ever
do that better than you
Levitate your spirit to
a higher level in life

and believe all can be yours

My Grandma use to tell me
"Pammy claim it and it's yours"
Allow no one to
take pure love
A real sense of the amour
for if it is in you
you know true magic

You know what it does
is the only answer
I don't feel this is tragic
Practice with great reality
how to leave
Your troubles
two blocks back

there is no other way
to keep on track
I heard a stillness
in the wind enter my soul
and told me to hold
and don't you let go
On you have only one soul

Do not let the ugliness
ruin your world
Turn your face to
the wind and feel the peace
that surround your
pearls and remember that no
one can do you better than you

Misunderstood Love

As I am sitting here
searching my true feelings
reaching out to feel
your soul touch mine
the bitter pain
of never ending memories
so sweet so cherished
a paradox inside
my tortured mind

a fury pushing
out of blindness reflects
the status of our endless love
a winding road channeled
through my mere emotions
leads my very essence
hopelessly untold
in my heart you
will always flourish

for the reality I knew
that blossomed from
the start an emptiness
that smolders deep within me
once forbidden now never
to be forgot
I will regret all
that was taken for granted
and remember the endearments
of our day

Millennium

I know your countenance
I smell your essence
I taste your being
I remember you
from the time before it was

I have traced the human race
to find some grace
and there you were
with warm embrace
hardships tribulations

and unexpected blows
only love keeeps me a glow
I have grown to live
on and enjoy the golden ages
through the pages

I am still here
I witness your faith
as time keeps ticking
in this mortal rage
we have labored hard

to keep changing
to be back one
with the Creator
a revolution of tears
a two edged sword

of cheers
again the anguish the poverty

of little ones tears
we were with the Creator
from the very start

he stirred the waters
blew first breath
through and through
all civilizations
and rebirth of many nations

rebirth us through tragedies
changing us to see clarity
I saw his face and you
were there waiting too see me

The Tree

once upon a spring began
life that desired to love
and to be loved
from that moment on
there blossomed forth
at the very essence
the planting of a seed

the tree of life
air's breath the spice ever
given free
facts of life
truth is light and advice is
given free
give it wise comfort's price
echoes of one's own peace

tree of life love's device divine

creation duplication
of Heavens glee
glow always flow always
precious nectar from
the fruit of the tree roots
are deep fruits promise
reaped the strongest limbs
in the wind will bend
And when the sun rose an

amorous show of rays
the mountain to gaze
the sky the attainable
high life's ascension
meant to be manifest
the dawn new kingdom come
spreading blessings adorned
by the King the Queen's

twilight stars shimmering bright
her son's wounded side
spills out in the night true stories
spout the cloudless droughts
what destiny forever good
those stories fall
from the tree that big or small
that sustains the life of you and me

There is a Revolution

there is a revolution of the spirit

that is transpiring the world

people who can only see the world
one way
they want it to be what they think

and never say what they know
in the preoccupation with the small
talk

ignorance of the mass
we can truthfully say that some

people have left its course and death
is ever after
to seize the moment of joy

rid the intelligence of self indulgence
pity we will learn to nurture
ourselves

get our lives back from the land of
the lost
we must take the opportunity to
laugh

when we feel the need to cry
to hold onto the good and rid the
self of temptation

to do bad look up with your head
touching the sky envelop and
embrace
the healing forces

that ride the constant waves
that fall from the rosy sun
I shall then sat satisfied that
humanity met with humility

not the woe of misfortune
chatter will be long behind us

no more small talk only the silence
of peace of mind
that follows all that matter in the
spirit

I dance, I dance, for all I dance, for
self
I dance for man,
ohm, I am woman, I am child
"I am that I am"

I am romance the true rhythm
a stroke of chance
I strike like lightening
I roar like thunder

I spit like rain there is a revolution
of the spirit that is transpiring the
world

Flowers and Weeds

In the field of life
we find many things
dirt stones grass and leaves

trees flowers birds and bees
but weeds
if you notice can be
a distraction of things

flowers they are pretty indeed
soft lovely spreading their essence
in the breeze
weeds on he other hand are trifling
to me intertwining whining
choking the life out of other beings
they make success hard finding

and began binding progress
in the garden of what
we are raising and need flowers
they support the trees
the stones the dirt the grass
the bees they want to help
the weeds but weeds
have different needs

weeds seem to have stubborn
greed choking smothering
killing all that has grown
from the seed Flowers
are a symbol of beauty
when they are properly sown

kind and always aware
of their duties brilliant
diversity colorful doing great
deeds in their deepest
corner of their heart

is determination to succeed

we all have choices in life
to be a flower or a weed
but once you know
you're a flower your life
becomes free to clearly seek

Fire Cracker

I wanted Summer to come and
when it came
it came so hot I couldn't hold it
the flame
the flame burn so high

I couldn't hold it teasing the flesh of
my face
it frightened me it felt l
like ants were eating my feet
escaping the summer heat depressed
me
but the coldest part of that hot
summer
was the heat that traveled with me

Let Me Dance

Let me dance
to the symphony of the universe
as fingered rays
play upon my strings I develop wings

and the orchestra flows with
the wind that press upon
my back the music then attack
I feel a storm within me

Rage of power that transforms
itself into the purest phase
of emotion to fashion an image of
goodness
A simplicity of thought as a young
child
complex as passion as hot
as true love between lovers
I roll with the waters tossing
me from one shore to the next

Let me dance, I shout praise
for the shedding of my discomfort
like that of a snake then recoiling
itself
to bring new life too old things
To viewing of life as if as the new
space
of a new place is already abound
saying thanks for the mercy and love
found

in the blades of grass springing back
after airy steps
dance happily on the roots I swirl
and then twirl with the vibration
of imaginative movement as
I look around and see smiling faces
applauding at my efforts to entertain

like the fruit that hangs
from the vine And I realize that I
am inseparable from the instruments
that plays me and the band that
sways me

The Advocate

We are tired
of running into the same thing
everyday
everywhere we go people that don't
care
taking up space of need filled chairs

when their light bulb is on simple
small things can improve and correct
the wrongs
we can get things right
meditate over new ideas these can be

things that turn things around
and benefit the maximum of happy
employment
with less waste less sick days and a
happy face
contagious place pull together as
community

then if only we'd here the moment of
silence
and restructure ourselves on a
personal basis

and go from there When we come
around
the energy of others as
we are giving and taking energy

After the daily grind in the evening
unwind
Learn to slow it down you'll be
astounded our stability grounded
and people not being heard start
complaining
Of course this can be aggravating

or one must speak out for their civil
rights.
Civil rights must be enforced in ones
own boarders of America
to get respect before we can go all
over
the world

telling them they and their
government is wrong.
And now we have the same thing at
home
We must recognize that we are
citizens
enforced by the law of the laws

Thread (the Quilt)

There is a light that guides us to seek
more of its' energy laughter

passion life when all about us
is like the storm of the ocean waves
the movement that stir waves

vast like those that capside a ship
hold our breath and dive into those
fierce waters only to find out that
we will arise from the moss into a
land
that once was a garden

We will know if it is truly time
to give the best of ourselves
no matter how big or small
My Grandma would say that "
we are no more than filthy rags"

A clay to mask the spirit that guides us
to our very freedom of people of
choice

so from this moment we cross
another bridge
with the opportunity of voice
to meet the world's needs our
brother's

and sister's our own a chance to
smile
in a globe of people that sometimes
feel they are the one and only
There are the common threads
that hold together all men and
women

for we are a quilt patched all in one
we are colorful and strong

Everyday

we must listen to the news
We learn who is at war
maybe why we are there
Maybe they will come here
statistics and public conversations
about politics

How many are making it
through a dying and injured
economy
The sacrifices of our families
Soldiers when they come home
there will be thoughts of everything
and every war
every political behavior every civil
right ignored

every disabilities act every soldier
whose loved one was whacked
every elderly, every single parent
whether the war was a just war or
not
the mere fact this man or woman
put their life on the line to get
where we have got

must sacrifice them for a while or
forever

There were programs set up of trusts
to be there when we all turned a
certain age
O.k. some things were not done right
they were not honest
are we going to usually takes
a lot more than the imagination
how horrible things can really be.

Fredrick Douglass
(the message)

The town was ruined as my dream
flew in
as if a rain storm of bombs fell from
above
there was no omen or representation
of a peaceful dove
as I look it's like hell pulverized
civilization to the ground
buildings devastated, the remains
are done
all is blown down

crushed like fine black pepper the
smell of distrust
in the air partnered with the dust
didn't seem that long ago
there was no rust nor the smell of
disgust filling the wall was a bust
surrounded
crumb pieces the size of croutons of
cement

rubble laying mixed within a large
clear

salad bowl without greens all
around
as if a large slice of bread torn the
screen on
the wall
Frederick Douglass is the man that
appeared
in a apart to make screen had there
been flesh
and as it has been blown away
except for this one wall standing
tall in the middle of what had
recently become
a land of no where hallowed

It was scarce
On this wall was a familiar face
my head deep
quickly remenencing intense his eyes
dark and deep
the wisdom and the intelligence
so steep in sorrow and tenacity
jacinth and boaz
fire in his eyes I have seen and
known
that exact portrait above
a bust of the chest to the bottom of
his trussels,

he said with no hesitation

He was speaking alot but all I could grasp
in what he was saying in a direct strong
confident voice,
"get to know the hearts of men"
the wall stood that had been a part of this city
with the looks of a black and white movie screen
hosting the reel to reel I knew this face

famous indeed "Get to know the hearts of men"
is what he looked me staight
in my eyes and said
Men wear many masks and styles of hats
with or without sin
sometimes they are translucent
and transparently thin
a few smooth tools and the psyche
will bend protect yourself
from those who are trying to get in

and other times muddy waters splash
how words are clouded
verve run astray the musical notes of
the blues come from living your life
colors come from the light spectrum
bending of all hues
Thus human beings we will know

the human by his heart
"get to know the hearts of men"

Murder in the First

Bought in shackles, culturally chained
held down bound
a product of society because it was
murder in the first degree
is there a special circumstance against me
bias racism liberalism right wing free thinkers
springing forth something that you cannot
begin to comprehend
strength cannot be held down
my ear is to the ground

listening to all that believe there is no sound
you conspired to murder my soul
seeking out methods
that had never been told not knowing
the snares in which you catch yourself
equality justice "OVER RULED" cried
the marionette puppet I see your face

no shine no glory no time no money
and no trial
only an unjust justice system content
to politicians
controlled by unawares that brag to
have no care

people are in despair naked mothers
with hungry children
on the stage to dance the money
dance and yet their bag
is still empty simply because of the
pimping of the master
of the game, jurist doctrine I already
have not something
I sold my soul for but, something I
reached out and grabbed
can you see that reality is the logic of
the truth
in understanding what life brings

what disservice you have done to
your fellow man?
No lies tied into a straightjacket of
redemption
truth is the only justice that rids the
ills that plague our lands
murder in the first is just a pomp in
circumstance
Uncanny choices broken voices old
tools beneath new hands
creating laws for the lonely man,
these men behind bars

are not the only beaten men open
your eyes and look

Or is the dust to thick upon your
book
all life has been special circumstance
an unstained heart tugged upon by
poison hands
your Simon says,"throw them off the
bridge",
you answer his command you do it
quick as possible
unbalanced empty headed man
but you see I have a soul that can't
be bought
I know you cannot entertain this
thought

like those before and those that may
come after you
around me they will always be
life for me has always been alone,
rather
the room was full or whether it was
empty
dark times to come were promised
only
to shed a little light it may be
murder
in the first but you won't take my
soul tonight

The Antedote

Everything necessary on this path
is already given to me
all I have to do is call
on the Lord and know
that he is my guide
when I have exhausted myself

trying to do things my way
the Holy Spirit takes over
and I receive the best rest
to receive and listen
to the message
and instead of trying

to do things my way
the Holy Spirit takes
over and receive the best
rest to receive and listen
to the message and then
he sends peaceful

people to assist
the Prophets has proclaimed
my path to show that God is real
and is all he uses us to Demonstrate
his truths good or bad and hear
on earh I am here that I may

receive our souls and establish
his establishment in God there is the
truth
all I must do is to believe and

profess his Holy name
nothing can harm me unless
God wants it too

my pains remind me that I
can get through anything
chastisement of the rod the staff
gives me the leaning arm of
the Lord to rest upon
and the power to perform his will

and miracles when we can't go on
relax and let God provide and then
trust
although the storm looks great l
ook for the good
and the miracles at hand
my enemies sees them all the time

because they
have sat the traps what they do not
understand
is how
I am still standing with my soul in
tact
and how
I am still moving toward

my mark with God
for he is laying everything
I truly need is in frront of me
and I shall feast in the bride
chamber
before them with my Lord

99

and they shall fall

You are emptying the old
for the new spirit and with
the alchemical marriage of your vessel
overflows with goodness
God will be with us all the days
of our lives and we shall

dwell in Heaven forever Amen
and so it is by declaration power of
the Omnipotent One and so it is

African Queen

woman wild strong as the jungle
vine
intoxicating getting better

aging like fine wine
slick as the city lights

bold as the summer soltice
sun that shine so bright

Queen reticent and aloof
female lionness shaved of hair

don't be scared
come into my lair

well true
I can devour you

like the sphinx in need of no riddle
my body is like the land of honey

rich milk
my river overflows like the nile

my land so fertile filling the world
with strong African Kings and
Queens

A future like the nile rough roaring
gentle yet strong that will never be
forgotten

now solve the riddle
soft classical music

Dream

Someday the world will listen
to the songs of nature calling to
awaken us to our
first state of being

the words will elevate us
out of a state of misery
the things of thought created from
chaos

notes of distant birds no longer
enslaving
our movements unbinding our souls
losing our minds

defining the times of a dark era

awakening the dawn and seeking
the sun
someday we will see our purpose and
heed the tides
the rhythmic waves upon the surface
of the murky grave

Lesson of Surrender

Today, I welcome surrender
I must give up my ego
looking forward to the rest of my life
Letting go,

detachment of a superficial place
is a momentary realness
questioned by time and dimension
space
War is for the Barbaric and the
ignorant, change?

What happened to greatness
A Civilized character that has
a mouth of great debate
without anger or doubt?

Emerald Green

For a stone peace of mind
In some situations you will find
that you are required to be at best
moving faster than the rest
has stone peace of mind

You are able to follow
that cobble stone road
looking for that moment of increase
beautification is the key to peace
will an emerald can be a jewel
that is so misunderstood because its
value runs steeper than its price

How the green plants and gems
affect the world we live in like those
born in May where the natural
pleasures
of play spring to summer brings
about love
and play when the natural kingdom
such as herbs and gems not ony heal
The green tourmaline and
adventurine
excites the attributes of the emerald
green

Wailing Wall Journal

Wailing Wall Journal

Wailing Wall Journal

Wailing Wall Journal

Wailing Wall Journal

Wailing Wall Journal

Wailing Wall Journal

Wailing Wall Journal

Wailing Wall Journal

Wailing Wall Journal

Wailing Wall Journal

Wailing Wall Journal

Wailing Wall Journal

Wailing Wall Journal

Wailing Wall Journal

Wailing Wall Journal

Wailing Wall Journal

Wailing Wall Journal

Wailing Wall Journal

Wailing Wall Journal

Wailing Wall Journal

Wailing Wall Journal

Wailing Wall Journal

Wailing Wall Journal

Wailing Wall Journal

Wailing Wall Journal

Wailing Wall Journal

Wailing Wall Journal

Wailing Wall Journal

Wailing Wall Journal

Wailing Wall Journal

Wailing Wall Journal

Wailing Wall Journal

Wailing Wall Journal

Wailing Wall Journal

Wailing Wall Journal

Wailing Wall Journal

Wailing Wall Journal

Wailing Wall Journal

Wailing Wall Journal

Wailing Wall Journal

Wailing Wall Journal

Wailing Wall Journal

Wailing Wall Journal

Wailing Wall Journal

Wailing Wall Journal

Wailing Wall Journal

Wailing Wall Journal

Wailing Wall Journal

Wailing Wall Journal

Wailing Wall Journal

Wailing Wall Journal

Wailing Wall Journal

Wailing Wall Journal

Wailing Wall Journal

Wailing Wall Journal

Wailing Wall Journal

Wailing Wall Journal

Wailing Wall Journal

Wailing Wall Journal

Wailing Wall Journal

Wailing Wall Journal

Wailing Wall Journal

Wailing Wall Journal

Wailing Wall Journal

Wailing Wall Journal

Wailing Wall Journal

Wailing Wall Journal

Wailing Wall Journal

Wailing Wall Journal

Wailing Wall Journal

Wailing Wall Journal

Wailing Wall Journal

Wailing Wall Journal

Wailing Wall Journal

Wailing Wall Journal

Wailing Wall Journal

Wailing Wall Journal

Wailing Wall Journal

Wailing Wall Journal

Wailing Wall Journal

Wailing Wall Journal

Wailing Wall Journal

Wailing Wall Journal

Wailing Wall Journal

Wailing Wall Journal

Wailing Wall Journal

Wailing Wall Journal

Wailing Wall Journal

Wailing Wall Journal

Wailing Wall Journal

Wailing Wall Journal

Wailing Wall Journal

Wailing Wall Journal

Wailing Wall Journal

Wailing Wall Journal

Wailing Wall Journal

Wailing Wall Journal

Wailing Wall Journal

Wailing Wall Journal

Wailing Wall Journal

Wailing Wall Journal

Wailing Wall Journal

Wailing Wall Journal

Wailing Wall Journal

Wailing Wall Journal

Wailing Wall Journal

Wailing Wall Journal

Wailing Wall Journal

Wailing Wall Journal

Wailing Wall Journal

Wailing Wall Journal

Wailing Wall Journal

Wailing Wall Journal

Wailing Wall Journal

Wailing Wall Journal

Wailing Wall Journal

Wailing Wall Journal

Wailing Wall Journal

Wailing Wall Journal

Wailing Wall Journal

Wailing Wall Journal

Wailing Wall Journal

Wailing Wall Journal

Wailing Wall Journal

Wailing Wall Journal

Wailing Wall Journal

Wailing Wall Journal

Wailing Wall Journal